TEA PARTY TALK
Connecting the Dots!

By
Senator H.L. "Bill" Richardson (RET)

TownhallPress

TEA PARTY TALK
Connecting the Dots!
by Senator H.L. "Bill" Richardson (RET)

Printed in the United States of America

ISBN 9781622302819

Dedication

To the pure joy of my life— my wife Barbara.

Table Of Contents

Foreword
by Pat Nolan

California State Assembly Republican Leader [1984 - 1988]

I pressed H.L. "Bill" Richardson to write *Tea Party Talk* because I had found his previous book *Slightly to the Right* so helpful in battling liberals. Bill has a unique ability to deconstruct the ploys that leftists use to change the discussion and distort facts to put conservatives on the defensive. I know that what you learn in this book will be helpful as you seek to convince your neighbors to support constitutional, fiscally responsible government in the upcoming elections.

The 2012 balloting promises to be the most consequential election since 1932. It was in the 1940's that Franklin Roosevelt turned the United States sharply to the Left towards socialism and the government has been growing exponentially ever since. The presidents who followed Roosevelt, both Republicans and Democrats, did not reverse the growth in government. Even under Ronald Reagan the federal government continued to expand. Under President Obama the cost of our government has grown exponentially.

The bill for this orgy of spending has finally come due. But with more people dependent on the government than those who support themselves, there are fewer people to pay off the mounting debt. The upcoming elections will determine whether we will be able to continue borrowing trillions to reshape our nation into a European welfare state, or the voters restrain the power and size of government and return it firmly within the bounds of the Constitution.

The battle for the presidency will be meaner and nastier than any in our lifetime. The far Left will not give up their power willingly.÷ One of the ways Americans can counter this leftist propaganda is over the backyard fence and the barbeque. Our message in support of constitutionally restrained, fiscally sound government will have to be delivered by each of us to our neighbors and friends.

The question is: *Will the Tea Party activists be able to present our case for liberty in a way that will win the public debate?* There is no question that we have truth and reason on our side. The challenge for the Tea Party will be to persuade our fellow citizens of the righteousness of our cause without turning them off with our fervor. *Tea Party Talk* will give you the tools to effectively argue for limited government. It will prepare you to recognize the tricks liberals use to change the subject and distort the facts. *Tea Party Talk* was written to prepare you for the battle; to show you the traps that liberals try to set for us with their appealing but illogical arguments, and there is no one more qualified to teach you than Bill Richardson.

Bill is truly a remarkable man. He is creative, articulate, and funny. He is also a brilliant political strategist and tactician. And most important, he has led conservatives to a string of victories in very tough elections. I have to admit I am a bit partial. Bill supported me when I challenged the establishment and ran for state Assembly on a "Cut taxes/Cut spending" platform. Most political observers said I didn't have a chance. In fact, one wag called my campaign "The Children's Crusade." But Bill endorsed me, provided much needed financial support, and dispatched his chief political strategist to advise my campaign.

When I took my seat in Sacramento, Bill became my mentor. He provided me a great example of being a congenial person while sticking to our conservative philosophy. He was gregarious and friendly to all, but he never let those relationships get in the way of his philosophy of limited government. He never joined the "go along to get along" crowd. I learned a great deal from him. I think when you read this book you will learn a great deal, too.

If you want to win back our government, Bill's book will prepare you for the fight better than anything else you will read. But don't take my word for it. Let Bill's record speak for itself. Bill was a highly successful advertising and marketing executive who got tired of having conservative positions misrepresented by the press and being sold out by his representatives in the state capitol. So, he left the private sector and ran for the state Senate. Against all odds he won the seat.

He arrived in the state Capitol in 1966 along with newly elected Governor Ronald Reagan to confront a state budget that was severely out of balance. Ronald Reagan paid eloquent tribute to Bill's service: "I know how much I counted on you when I was Governor."

After his election, Bill quickly observed that the Republicans were not only outnumbered, but many of his fellow GOPers had simply stopped fighting. Bill decided to change the equation, and over the next few years he founded five separate PAC's to elect more conservatives. He not only took on the liberals, but he got involved in primaries to support the more conservative candidates. Through his aggressive involvement in elections, Bill moved the legislature to the right and made the Republican Caucuses more assertive of our philosophy. In 1978, the year that the voters slashed property taxes with Proposition 13, Bill supported a whole group of solid conservatives including me.

Once the "Class of Prop. 13" conservatives supported by Bill reached the Capitol in 1978, not a single tax increase was approved during the rest of Bill's tenure. And when a surplus developed, over $1 billion was rebated to the tax payers, cutting the base on which future budgets would be established. You should have heard the liberals howl.

California's Supreme Court was pushing the state further and further left. Bill's Law and Order Campaign Committee led the fight against the retention of the very liberal Chief Justice, Rose Bird, and several of her associate justices. When the dust settled Bird was defeated by more than a million votes, as were two other liberals associate justices.

Two of the most effective groups Bill organized were Gun Owners of America and Gun Owners of California. GOC fought against an initiative that proposed to ban new sales of handguns in the state. Through direct mail, Bill alerted gun enthusiasts around the state to the danger of the initiative. Bill set up a coordinated effort with the NRA and the California Rifle and Pistol Association, with Bill directing the overall campaign. Bill's efforts were so successful that not only was the initiative defeated, the absentee voters Bill recruited provided enough votes to carry the Governorship for the Republican, who had lost among the voters who cast their ballots on election day. The tidal wave of absentee ballots from gun owners across the state swept him into office.

I mention all this because Bill not only knows how to talk a good game - he knows how to win the important fights. And with all that is at stake in this presidential election, Bill's sound advice will prepare you for the vicious tactics that the Obama team will employ.

I let my son read *Tea Party Talk* last year when he was a senior in high school. He texted me in the middle of the day, "Teacher tried to change the subject just like Bill said he would. I nailed him!" I guarantee that after reading *Tea Party Talk* you will recognize the tactics of the left and deftly parry their lies and distortions, and appear pretty intelligent to the rest of those listening. That is how the grassroots will help win the Presidency, and restore constitutional government to the United States. (signed *Pat Nolan, March, 2012*)

Introduction

Have you ever found yourself with your back against a wall, trying to disengage yourself from a one-sided debate with one of your liberal acquaintances? All you did was say that you were pretty upset with large governmental debt, socialism in our government, and the lousy political leadership.

Before you could hardly say another word, you found yourself being put on the defensive, in the position of being against almost everything and everybody, including baseball, apple pie, and mom.

You are not alone. It's happened to me as well. To clarify the score, I bet you love apple pie, played a pretty hot game of baseball, and who doesn't like their mother?

But to hear my "friend" tell it, I was "against" and not "for." I didn't care about the downtrodden, the homeless, the aged and callously implied that I wanted to see the "underprivileged" starve to death.

It wasn't long before I started to feel my ears tingle as the blood angrily rushed to my head—my tongue was incoherently wagging in desperate defense, and I had the uncontrollable urge to smack 'em right in their smirking, smiling, collectivist countenance. At this moment, sensing my impending overt frustrated rage, he decided that the debate would soon turn into physical combat, so he dismissed himself from my presence with a wave of his hand and a scurrilous parting shot of: "Oh, well, it's all relative anyway!" Gad, was I mad!

Later, in my car driving home, I was still mentally smarting from the debate. I had a deep sense of frustration because I darn well cared about hungry people and resented being pushed into this position of being against everything. What made matters worse, this wasn't the first time, but it certainly was the worst going-over to which I had been subjected.

Why? I asked myself that question time and time again—I knew my facts, so why did I always find myself on the defensive? I then started, for the first time, to observe other such debates more analytically. I began to notice some simple and all too obvious techniques that my verbal opponents have been using on me for years. I started to employ these techniques as I became aware of them, and all of a sudden I started winning arguments with the very same people who had used me as their prime target for verbal "kicks." In fact, after a while I even started converting some of them.

What I will be discussing in this book will not be a classical debate system under the Marquis of Arguesbury rules where each person has five minutes to state his views and then the rebuttal, but the kind of conversational weapons you need in everyday discussions where you hope to convince your friends that our nation is in serious trouble.

Undoubtedly you have found that knowing your facts and proving your point with documentation doesn't necessarily guarantee a sale. How you present your position and your understanding of the person to whom you are speaking is almost as important as your information. Ask yourself, "How many times have I been irrefutably right on a matter and yet unable to convince the other person?"

> "How many times have I been irrefutably right on a matter and yet unable to convince the other person?"

One thing I hope this book will do is shed a little light on how you can better communicate with your friends who are less informed than you on the subjects of socialism, communism and welfare-statism.

If you are tired of being "shot down" in arguments by your "slightly to the left" friends, this book will give you guide-lines on how to win these discussions and, at the same time, not lose your friends. In fact, you might make converts out of some of them.

Sound impossible? Not at all if you are willing to take a little criticism objectively and read this book with the thought of gaining knowledge instead of receiving an emotional kick. Practice what you learn and you can improve your ability to communicate. Tired of talking to yourself? Then do something about it!

Chapter One

Good Guys Always Win?

November 4, 1964. The sun shone brightly over Southern California, but over the more than one hundred "Goldwater for President" headquarters hung little clouds of gloom, easily seen by the discerning. What happened? For the first time since we-couldn't-remember-when, we felt we had everything going for us. We had conservative workers in the precincts, poll watchers, victory squads, and we thought we had all the paraphernalia necessary for victory. We had a candidate who was a straight shooter (not from the hip, that is) or, as the Indians would say, a man who didn't speak with a forked tongue. He was a man of principle and proven integrity, and to top it all off, he was good-looking. We had facts and figures coming out of our ears, educational material on our candidate by the boat-load, enthusiasm, boola-boola, not to mention zis-boom-bah.

We thought our opposition was ideal. The Democrat candidate for president had been on both sides of the issues so often that it was unbelievable. Lyndon Johnson's record was so up-and-down that he was referred to as Yo-Yo Bird. His running mate, Hubert Humphrey, was even more unbelievable. Johnson's public record as an avowed southpaw could leave no doubts in anybody's mind. In fact, those who didn't believe it had only to ask him and he would proudly boast of it. His long public record of promoting socialism and "big daddy" government was common knowledge to we conservatives, and his praises were constantly being sung by contraltos of the Norman Thomas school of socialistic songbirds and the media.

So, in all good conscience, we put two and two together and figured we had a winner. We felt it in our bones. "Good guys always win." We were conscious of a general public awareness of all these factors (so we thought). We certainly had taken the message into the precincts. We felt that the American people were capable of rational thought and if presented with a "Choice, Not an Echo," a choice would be made. We could justifiably prove that this was not a matter of partisan politics; in fact, it was a matter of national survival. The issues crossed over political boundaries into the arena of what was best for our beloved America.

So, with verve and rugged tenacity, we threw ourselves into the fray, confident that Americans of all political beliefs would "rally around the flag," "Onward, upward, straight shooters," "Don't give up the ship," "Morality forever," "Better dead than red," "Over the top, boys!" You name it, we said it, and meant it, too!

Late in the evening about midnight of November 3, we sat all huddled around the "boob tube" watching the results come pouring in. We were by that time in a state of suspended shock. We watched the "objective" commentators gleefully reporting the vote tally, savoring every new result before they shared the "glad tidings" with us.

After a while, I couldn't take it any more, so I gravitated into the kitchen to pour myself a drink. For a moment I considered Hemlock on the rocks or Arsenic and tonic with a twist, but finally decided on a milder concoction. I found a sour mash made in one of the states that went for Goldwater and poured myself a healthy one. I am not a drinking man by and large, but that night it wouldn't have made any difference anyway. I was so numb that I doubt if even the Hemlock on the rocks would have affected me.

The doorbell rang; other friends started to arrive at our home for the wake. Before long a large number of gloomy-faced friends had gathered in the den, and, in typical fashion, we started to contemplate what went wrong. What should we do? *Form a suicide pact, ride the decline, or fight again?*

The comments came fast and heavy. Strong opinions mark informed people, and they are almost never hesitant in stating them.

"What's wrong with people, can't they **see** what's happening?"
"Boy, are we in for it!"
"They **deserve** slavery!"
"Pass the tonic!"
"Why are people so dumb... couldn't they see the difference?"
"Aw... they just don't care!"
"Everybody wants a handout."
"I'm disgusted with people."
"Where's the ice?"
"It's just like Rome in the last years...we're on the decline."
"Everybody's been brainwashed!"
"Gee, I thought I had my precinct."

It went on into the wee hours. In the background the constant drone of the television reported the ever-increasing size of the defeat; now and then a congressional race was reported with the same devastating results.

We had been soundly defeated. Why?

> We awakened many people to the threat of socialism.

Good guys always win? It usually works that way in the movies, especially if the hero happens to be Clint Eastwood, John Wayne or Harrison Ford; but in real life who often wins? Often in politics there isn't really a choice in the general presidential election; sometimes you're given the choice between two of the same birds with slightly different verbal plumage.

In 1964 we had the right candidate in the general election, but the mainstream media and the left wing democrats projected us to the general public as the "NO" side of the ticket. "NO on aiding the poor, NO on organized labor, NO on abortion, NO on funding education, and negative on everything else."

The media was right on calling us "NO" but they chose the wrong no's. We had no talk radio, no national conservative organizations of size, no internet, no conservative blogs, no national means of substance to tell our story to a national audience, and little knowledge on how to win battles with the hard left.

Oh, yes—and we had no national grass roots movement like the Tea Party. But what we did have was the awakening by a segment of Americans to a real threat to our freedoms and a desire to get organized. In 1964 conservative politics was in its infancy, even the grass roots was green as grass. We were enthusiastic to the point of being scary; our communication skills needed refining and retooling and in our fervor we scared as many as we converted. However, much good came out of our failed attempt to elect Goldwater. We awakened many people to the threat of socialism and one of Goldwater's most effective spokesman was elevated to national political prominence—a Hollywood actor by the name of Reagan.

Just two years later, in 1966, we conservative Californians helped Reagan overwhelmingly defeat a former RINO mayor of San Francisco in the Republican primary for Governor and then overwhelmingly defeat Governor Brown in the general election.

Doesn't the Lord work in strange, mysterious, and wondrous ways?

Chapter Two

Inspect Yourself!

There's an old political axiom that, "You learn more from your defeats than your victories." In many ways this is true, but this expression certainly cannot be categorized as a truism.

Conservatives have been losing elections and discussions for years and the "Liberals" have been winning. You might think that we would learn from our past defeats and win for a change, but unfortunately that hasn't been the case. By this time if "learning from our past defeats" were true, we should be mental giants.

There is another old expression which is much more apropos: "A fox always smells his own burrow first." In other words, before we start blaming everybody else, let's look at ourselves; or as the Chinese sage Sun Tsu said, "The clue to winning is know yourself as well as you know your enemies." Think carefully about that very wise statement. How well do we know how our country's enemies think—and, then how they act verbally? And, how well do we understand how our thoughts control our verbal actions?

First of all Americans are sometimes poor communicators. Sometimes I think we would have trouble selling whale blubber to a rich starving Eskimo. Because of our basic nature, we think that all we have to do is speak the truth and the sale is made. We are constantly being shocked out of our shoes by friends who not only reject what we say, but look upon us as a group of squirrels gathering nuts. Some of us are as welcome in social gatherings as the bubonic plague. I can speak from a position of authority because of my past experiences. There was a time when I would go to a cocktail party, walk into the house and stare at an empty room. I swear people would evaporate into the woodwork to avoid me. They stopped asking: "What's new, Bill?" because I would, in no uncertain terms, tell them.

It took a while before I finally had the sense to ask myself, "Say, maybe I'm approaching this all wrong." Had I been practicing conservative dialectics: *one step forward, two steps back?* Upon reflection I concluded, I hadn't been putting all the proper conversational and emotional dots together in how to influence my friends.

Introspection is a difficult task. It is difficult to admit mistakes once you find them, and often difficult to correct them. For myself, it's been a painful process, but the pain is more than offset by the gain from this self-inspection. I discovered getting the dots lined up in proper order can be very rewarding.

> "Know yourself as well as you know your enemies."

Talking to somebody isn't necessarily communicating. We have all talked to people, but talking obviously hasn't been enough. Unfortunately, the other person has to listen. If talking were enough, we would have won long ago. The tongue is a two-edged sword. You can talk people into believing you or, through what you say (and how you say it), you can drive people away.

What does communication mean to our nation's enemies? *A great deal.* In fact, through their ability to communicate ideas and disguise their programs, and by controlling certain facets of the communications media, they have been attempting to lead this country's citizens down the road to socialism. The fantastic amount of attention that the Communists and Socialists give to the propaganda media should make all of us wonder: *why do they give it such importance?* Let's briefly investigate what communication means to them and what effect they wish it to have upon us.

Chapter Three

Controlled Communications

Deception and guile are tactics that have been used since the devil induced Eve to stick an apple under Adam's nose. Unfortunately, people have been biting on Satan's fruit ever since. Down through history devious men have used trickery as a tool of war, politics and business. The Trojans with their horse outside the gates yelling, "There ain't nobody here but us cowboys," to the socialists in congress with their, "There ain't nobody here but us Blue dogs," to Obama telling us he's going to shrink the deficit by spending more trillions.

> The dissemination of controlled propaganda is a cold, calculated, mathematical science!

In the distant past, propaganda was used with hit-and-miss effectiveness. In today's world, the dissemination of controlled propaganda is a cold, calculated, mathematical science— analytically tested and retested. It is a studied art, a central and dominant factor in business, politics—and especially in dictatorial movements planning world conquest.

To ignore or be unaware of strategic use of propaganda as an effective tool of war is literally committing national suicide. To believe that you, the reader, have not in one way or another been affected by this science is the height of naivety. We all have been affected by it, Conservative, Liberal, and Independent alike.

I became well aware of the studied manipulation of communications early in my professional life. Before becoming engaged in politics, I was in the advertising world as both a commercial artist and as an account executive, dealing with national advertising agencies on a daily basis. Communications was my business and its study has been a lifetime endeavor. It is a fascinating and frightful experience, especially when you become aware of how it's been effectively used by America's enemies—both foreign and domestic.

It would be impossible in one book to go into all the facets of propaganda and psychological warfare because of the broadness of the subject, but it is important that we briefly touch upon one phase—Cybernetic Warfare.

The word "Cybernetics" is derived from the Greek "Kybernetike," which means the art of steer-man-ship. In other words, to steer or control. To the hard left; the socialist, humanist, and especially the international communist movement, cybernetics means to control or steer communications in such a manner as to achieve specific results in promoting their power grab.

> Cybernetics means to control or steer communications in such a manner as to achieve specific results!

Cybernetics is the science of giving controlled doses of propaganda to a broad sector of the population without their knowledge. The intention is to condition people to react in a given manner at a given signal.

The radical left, through a long, slow process of patient infiltration, has been laying a foundation for manipulation of the information Americans receive.

Ask yourself the following question, "If conspirators wanted to take over our country and knew they couldn't do it militarily at this time, wouldn't the manipulation of communications to soften and weaken America be an important factor?" The answer is obvious.

Pavlovian Dogs

Where did the Communist/Socialists get the idea in the first place of controlling people through this form of brainwashing? Edward Hunter, probably the world's foremost authority on brainwashing, stated:

> *The basis for modern psychological warfare, which makes it different from whatever was done in the past, are the findings of the Russian physiologist, Pavlov. He was not a Communist. He had completed his most important discoveries before the Communists took power. His first discovery was the effectiveness of using a living animal in experiments, rather than a dead animal. His second great discovery was that the instincts of an animal, which we call reflexes, were of two kinds. One was the reflexes which the animal was born with, it's unconditioned reflexes. The other was its conditioned reflexes, which man can train into the animal. Most of us have heard of Pavlov's experiments with dogs and lights. He first provided a bowl of food and turned on a light of a certain color, then an empty bowl and turned on a different colored light. After he had done this a number of times, he turned on the light that accompanied the food, but presented an empty bowl to the animal, and the dog deposited just as much saliva as when the bowl was full. When he presented a bowl full of food with the wrong light, the animal did not eat."[1]*

By this time you are probably wondering, what does a salivating mongrel have to do with me? Let's continue the quote and see.

> *After he had switched the lights and the bowls of food, the dog became neurotic, barked, and was driven into a state which among human beings we call insanity... When the Communist hierarchy in Moscow discovered that it was unable to persuade people willingly to follow Communism, when they found they could not create what they wanted, the 'new Soviet man' in which human nature would be changed, they turned to Pavlov and his experiments. They considered people the same as animals anyway and refused to recognize the roll of reason or divinity in the human being. They took over the Pavlovian experiments on animals and extended them to people. They did so with the objective of changing human nature and creating a 'new Soviet man.'* **People, they anticipated, would react voluntarily under Pavlovian pressures, in the way the dog does, to Communist orders, exactly as ants do in their collectivized society.**[2]

The last sentence really gives us an insight into the Communist interest in communications. Instead of lights as Pavlov used them to condition animals, Communists are using communications to condition us. It has been over a hundred years since Pavlov's original experiments, and the Communists have progressed substantially since then in their refinement of this Pavlovian process. In other words, to take over a country that's stronger, infiltrate and subvert the communications and educational processes of the enemy. Thus, over a sustained period of time, one gains control of the information he receives. When you have conditioned (educated) and programmed him sufficiently to react for, or against, whatever you choose, it is then just a matter of time until he is in your power.

Usually at this point someone will say: "Well, Jocko, that sounds great in theory, but it can't happen here. It's impossible to take over all of the communications in a country as large as America." In part, that is right. It would be practically impossible to take over **all** communications, but they don't need **all**, just key positions.

Let me give a few examples of how it could work. Television Station PDQL has on its staff a typical group of commentators, no dumber or brighter than any other sector of the professional community. Their news coverage has definitely given the impression of being extremely biased favoring "big daddy" government. It is natural to assume that the commentators themselves **must** know what they are doing, but this isn't necessarily the case.

Every TV Station has a dispatch desk. The dispatcher in Station PDQL sends the reporters out to cover certain assignments that the dispatcher deems newsworthy. In this particular station the dispatcher, more than 80% of the time, sends the reporters to interview only those of strong left-wing persuasion. Over a period of years the station's commentators naturally become more and more indoctrinated and the viewing audience is led to the left.

Another example: Station RUCK has the same type of commentators, and it too gives the definite left-wing slant all of the time. Only this time it's not the dispatcher; it's the film editor who is playing hanky panky with the computer programming.

> "Ignorance ain't our problem, it's all we know that ain't true."
>
> ~ Will Rogers

A journeyman reporter, with cameraman and crew, receives an assignment to interview a conservative Congressman who opposes the concept of a socialist government. The interview lasts five minutes. The man states his position clearly and accurately. The crew then departs to interview the other side of the argument and tapes again for five minutes. Now back to the studio. The film editor scans the ten minutes of interviews, and happily goes to work with his computer. The best of the conservative's statements wind up deleted and the best of the leftist's are seen by the viewing audience.

It is best at this time to remember again Will Rodger's comment. "Ignorance ain't our problem; it's all we know that ain't true."

Another example: Let's say this time a dedicated leftist worms his way into a strategic information position within our government.

Many of the legitimate newsmen depend upon reliable information from government officials to keep the public informed about our Nation's affairs. This leftist official takes it upon himself to "manage" news so that it won't embarrass his particular department. Uncomplimentary statistics are easily forgotten and complementary ones are widely distributed to the press.

We're getting a large dose of misinformation from politicians in Washington on how deep the financial hole the bureaucracy has dug for the taxpayers. "In debt? Why worry, we owe it all to ourselves!" (And we owe the Chinese Communists, too.]

Mainstream Media Ain't Objective

Herb Philbrick served nine years in the Communist apparatus for the F.B.I. as a Counter Agent for our government. One of the segments of the Communist structure he worked within was the Agit-Prop (agitation-propaganda) division. Mr. Philbrick has repeatedly warned Americans to be aware of Communist effectiveness in manipulating communications.

All too often we think that the socialist spends all of their time telling lies. That's not necessarily true. You can be brainwashed to a certain viewpoint by what you **don't** hear almost as much as by what you do hear. Omission is a strategic weapon and almost impossible to detect. If Americans could accurately see both sides of the question, communism and socialism wouldn't be around today. If most Americans were even slightly aware of the deviousness and historical brutality of communist nations, they wouldn't tolerate the present situation. But, unfortunately, most Americans don't comprehend the insidious nature of the beast. This general lack of knowledge of the international conspiracy isn't accidental, it's planned.

In the above examples you have seen how just a few people properly placed, can effect fantastic control over communications. The Socialists and Communists understand this all too well, and are constantly working toward this goal of

> Omission is a strategic weapon and almost impossible to detect.

total manipulation of communications. As the Communists have stated, "Comrade, one person in the right place at the right time is all we need."

In communications, as in any of our major institutions, a few properly placed enemies can do tremendous damage. Americans must understand that the radical left has been infiltrating our media for a long time. As an example, in the late 1930s Whitaker Chambers had been a hard core communist for many years. He gave testimony before the House Committee on Un-American Activities in 1939. Before the House Committee and in his book "Witness" he said, "There is probably no important magazine or newspaper in the country that is not Communist penetrated to some degree."[3]

Isn't that a shocking statement? Unfortunately, our nation's enemies are plural, alive, calculating, and have been at work for a long time. Today, we are faced with multiple enemies: Islamic extremists, Socialists, and those who I believe are the most dangerous, the cadre who adhere to international communist doctrine. Each cadre member, no matter in what country in which they reside, are dedicated to the destruction and the overthrow of The United States of America. They are at war with us.[4]

Remember, it doesn't take two to make a war; enmity only has to exist in the mind of one and we are at war whether we like it or not. Marxist Leninist doctrine has declared war to the death with us. It is a basic fundamental belief of every communist in every country world-wide, including America. Slow patient gradualism always has been one of their methods. They believe time and history are on their side—Karl Marx said so.

Poppycock! To rephrase Will Rodgers, "Ignorance ain't their problem. It's all the communists know that ain't true." History tells us, that over time, freedom is on the rise, not slavery.[5]

Americans are waking up to the obvious fact that the major media sometimes doesn't give us all the facts and there are a number of things we "know" that aren't true. Like the main street media ain't objective. However, thank God that most Americans aren't dumb. Quite a few of us have a fair degree of common sense and given time, most can figure out that two plus two is four, especially when the main stream media keeps telling us the answer is five.

Also, the media is trying to convince us that our next door neighbors and friends, who happen to belong to the local tea party, are a bunch of right wing screwballs. We know better, two and two is still four.

In this twenty-first century, Americans are waking up to the fact that the main stream media, by blowing hard from the left, has forced our ship of state into dangerous waters. If it hadn't been for the fair wind blowing from talk radio, FOX News and the Internet, we would be dangerously close to going under.

The liberal Democrats, elected in the 2006 and then taking control of both houses and the presidency in the 2008 elections, scared the pants off of many Americans. Their greatest accomplishment to date was galvanizing many sleepy citizens into patriotic action. One day it may well be said in jest that President Obama, unintentionally, by shocking Americans out of their skivvies and into action, has saved America. If it happens, let's build him a statue...with two attached teleprompters.

Okay, we may personally have a slight communications problem, right? Now, in the next chapter, we will discover what we can do about it.

Chapter Four

Ask Questions

A man from Massachusetts was once asked: "Why do you people from Massachusetts always answer a question with a question?"

The man from Massachusetts replied: "What do you mean we always answer a question with a question?"

You would think that all Liberals came from Massachusetts after analyzing that joke. How many times have you been in a discussion with a Fuzzy Liberal on some important subject, and before you could bat your eye, found yourself on another subject, then another, and another, ad infinitum? Pretty soon you get the definite impression that he thinks you are against apple pie, baseball, and Mom.

What has happened is that your friend hasn't responded **at all** to your original point or **statement**. He has, in turn, fired a question at you, and while you are trying to answer the question he's asked, your Fuzzy friend has already re-loaded his vocal cannons to fire another question at you.

It doesn't take long before your dander starts to rise, the hair on the back of your neck bristles, and your blood pressure soars.

You have fallen, as usual, into a typical semantic trap where you find you're in a defensive position and losing control of the discussion.

Let's take a typical situation and analyze it. You're at work and you make the statement, "Say Charlie, America is up to its neck in debt. The Democrats have been bankrupting the country at a rapid rate. We've got to do something about it."

Charlie responds: "What do you mean the Democrats? Don't you think Bush had something to do with it? Do you go along with the way the poor and our old folks are suffering from lack of proper medical attention?" (Change subject, change emphasis, ends in a question).

"Why are you right-wingers opposed to Obama-care and helping our sick citizens?"

"Obama-care! It's socialism pure and simple" (Statement again) says the conservative.

Your friend then replies: "What do you have against our elected representatives? They voted for it didn't they. What's the matter, are you against our government? What makes you think you're smarter than our elected officials?" (Questions) And on and on and on...

The conservative, because of his nature and education, has read a lot about our monetary problems and is angered about the administrations rush into more socialist programs while ignoring our national debt, but within fifteen seconds after he broaches the subject he finds himself portrayed as against everything and an oppressor of the elderly.

The conservative unknowingly has just been subjected to left-wing techniques by a friend who **probably doesn't even know he is using them.**

Many American liberal's argumentative nature is to systematically fire questions at the conservatives. These questions are geared to put him in a defensive position, and unfortunately the conservative unknowingly allows it to happen.

Why does he allow this to take place? Why is he constantly

back-tracking instead of going on the offense?

There are many reasons. Let's name a few.

First, the Conservative has a strong moral foundation. He has a code of ethics by which he evaluates all he hears and reads. Based upon this knowledge of right and wrong, he naturally comes to conclusions which he invariably expresses as statements, not questions.

Second, the conservative doesn't like being evasive; he's been asked a question and feels compelled to answer. He usually argues in a predetermined manner, based upon his prior conditioning and thus he is easily side-tracked.

Third, when a person is making statements, he has to slow his mind down to the speed of the spoken word, and hence he is easily manipulated by the person who is asking the questions. A person listening can think at least three times as fast as the one who is talking. In other words, a person's mind is often three times faster than his mouth.

> A person's mind is often three times faster than his mouth.

Fourth, the conservative has argued defensively for so long it has become an ingrained habit pattern. It is a bad habit which we must break.

Fifth, the Liberal feels no compulsion to answer a direct question, many of them think that everything's "relative" anyway. The habit of asking questions is inculcated in him or her; hence, Liberals are always on the offensive (anti-conservative). The conservative is not. (If you don't believe me, strike up **any** conversation on **any** political subject and watch the cliché questions come flowing out of your Liberal friend's mouth).

There are other reasons and we will cover them in other chapters, but let's concentrate on how we can go on the offensive.

Ask Questions

Develop the habit—**I repeat, develop the habit**—of asking questions instead of making statements. If you make a statement, learn how to tack on a question such as, "What do you think of that?" **Keep them on the subject you want to talk about.** Smile, and gently bring them back to the subject you started with, like "don't you think the country is in deep debt?"

Questioning a person can accomplish many things:

- You can ascertain the degree of knowledge the person has at his command on any given subject. How are you, as a conservative, going to educate unless you establish wheAre the education process has to start? How many times have you talked to people about "foreign aid to socialist nations" and found out later that the person didn't even know what socialism is? You have to ascertain the degree of knowledge your friend has, and the only way is to draw him out by asking questions.

- You control the subject matter and thus the conversation. (More on this in the next chapter)

The person being questioned has to think! Only through posting a series of questions can you break through the comfortable wall of clichés so many of our friends have erected around their brain cells; clichés that have been conveniently supplied to them by the collectivist planners. You have to break through their surface knowledge.

Let me give you an example of how it works. Three people were having lunch; one fuzzy liberal, two conservatives. The conservatives were talking about communism. Before long the liberal couldn't take it anymore and came pouring into the conversation with both left feet.

> **Keep them on the subject you want to talk about.**

"Don't you know you're all wrong?" he emphatically asks, "I read the daily papers. Don't you think the media—*Time, Newsweek,* and *The New York Times*—keeps up on all of this? Where do you get your conclusions? They're contrary to what I read. Are these publications all wrong?"

At this point the conservatives could have answered typically with, "Those publications! Do you believe **those** liberal rags? Do you know that...."

Fortunately they didn't but if they had then the conservatives would have been put into the position of being "against." To the Liberal they would have been attacking one of America's most cherished institutions, the free press. They would have reacted typically, and from that point on nothing positive would have been accomplished.

Instead, one of the conservatives turned to the liberal and said, "Gee, I'm glad that you know all about communism. I've had trouble understanding the dialectic mind of the communist. Would you explain it to me?"

"Huh?" stammered the liberal.

"Well then," inquired the conservative, "what do you think is the most dangerous communist transmission belt in our State?"

"Communist transmission belt? Do they make automotive parts too?" asked the surprised liberal.

"No, a transmission belt is a front which is used to pass on communist propaganda to the uninformed public," stated the conservative. "Which front do you think is doing the most damage?"

By this time the liberal was totally confused, "I guess I don't know as much about communism as I thought I did," he honestly admitted. "How do these transmission belts work?" he asked.

Now he was actually listening to the conservatives and not reacting.

The conservatives posed questions. They didn't react. They controlled the conversation, pointed out to their friend his lack of knowledge on the subject of communism, and intelligently won his attention.

The day conservatives develop the ability to ask questions and go on the offensive will be the day we really start rolling back socialism and communism.

All it takes is practice and patience. Are you willing?

Chapter Five

Trigger Words

We obviously use words to communicate with each other. But what happens when the average words we use when addressing our fellow Americans aren't understood or think they mean something else? When we group words together in a well-arranged order, they serve as a bridge of understanding between people, but that only happens when words don't change their meanings. As long as their meanings remain consistent we can communicate with each other. If the meanings of all words were in a constant state of flux, the communication of ideas would be impossible. It has been stated that: "When man loses understanding and a proper relationship to his words he loses touch with reality."

Confusing the meaning of words is now a studied applied science, and specifically used by enemies of our country to confuse segments of our population; while at the same time relaying specific instructions to their party faithful. I'm now speaking specifically of the international communist movement. These buggers haven't changed their goal of world conquest—not one iota. In fact they are stronger and more powerful than they have ever been. Therefore, their use of language as a tool of conflict and conquest continues. They refer to it as "Aesopian" or "sectarian" Language. It is quite simply—semantic weaponry.

Dr. Stefan T. Possony, a recognized authority on Communist semantic tricks, stated:

> *Every Communist communication must convey an orthodox, that is, revolutionarily activating message to the party and its followers. This same communication must convey a different, soothing, pacifying, and paralyzing message to the opponent of communism."[6]*
>
> *Communists, have, over a period of years,... cleaned up the language which they addressed to the non-initiated[7] ... change meanings of words, confuse, destroy their meanings, and through this semantic weaponry, condition people. The communist message should be couched in terms which have a positive ring in the ears of the audience. Communism must be dressed up as something like democratic liberalism or patriotic nationalism. Offensive and locally unfamiliar terms must be avoided... any good communist would now be able to use language which is not to be found in the classical writings of Marx and Lenin but occurs*

> When man loses understanding and a proper relationship to his words he loses touch with reality.

in Jefferson, Mill or Jane Addams.[8]

"Revolution" became "liberation," and the physical extermination of entire groups of people, "classes," and nations became the "laying of the foundations of socialism." Occasionally, even the word "communism" disappeared from the vocabulary and was replaced by "anti-fascism" or, more recently, "anti-imperialism"... Lenin, who invented, among communists, those tactics of language, occasionally even abandoned the use of his favorite word, "revolution"; instead, he talked about the reform, which he contrasted to reforms.[9]

In conversations with friends who are not well informed on semantic chicanery, you will find you may have to continually define words so that you both understand one other. This is especially true in any conversation that you might have on politics or when discussing socialism or communism. Many Americans have accepted new meanings of certain words and phrases which in the classic interpretation would be incorrect. As an example, let's take the word "conservative." The dictionary defines a political conservative as:

1. A person tending to preserve from ruin or injury.

2. One who aims to preserve from innovation or radical change; one who wishes to maintain an institution or form of government in its present state.

From this definition you **might** call us conservatives because we want to conserve the constitutional structure as it was intended, but we have no intention of conserving some of our present programs such as deficit spending and endless growth of welfare. From the classical definition of the word, the epitome of liberal morality, the Arkansas philanderer Bill Clinton would be a Conservative. Why? Because he and others of the same political persuasion are not only trying to "conserve" but increase our federal bureaucracy by trillions of dollars.

"Conservative" to present day conservatives usually means one who loves his country and its institution, opposes totalitarianism, believes in individual freedom, is not selfish or bigoted, embraces other people's interests, and advocates greater freedom of thought and action. Don't get "shook," but I have just given you Webster's Dictionary definition of "liberal." If you don't believe me, look it up.

> **Never assume that the person to whom you are speaking defines words exactly as you do.**

"Conservatism" to socialists and communists means one thing only—active opposition, or as they call it—Fascism.!

"Conservatism" to the laboring man generally gives rise to anti-labor thoughts.

"Conservatism" to the Socialist means opposition to a planned economy.

Never assume that the person to whom you are speaking defines words exactly as you do, especially if he holds different political views.

We often assume that people understand the terminology we use. If you are talking to a labor union man who reads and believes only Union publications, he could think Conservatives are death warmed over, and if in a conversation with this man you say, "I'm a Conservative and proud of it," and you assume that he feels the same way about the word "Conservative" as you do, you've made a grave mistake. He, in all probability, believes that **you** have the same conception of the word "Conservative" as **he** does. In other words, he probably thinks, "Why this so-and-so is anti-Labor and proud of it!"

Here are a few of the words that practically all hard leftists use and their definitions:

Fascist -   *An active, effective anti-Communist, anti Socialist bigot.*

Right Winger -	*One who works against an anti-socialist government.*
Co-existence -	*A temporary situation until the communists gain time to infiltrate, subvert and gain strength.*
Peace -	*The final victory over Capitalism and the conquest of America.*
Democracy -	*A one-world socialist state under Communist rule.*
Emerging Nations -	*Nations that throw off Feudalism and gravitate towards a Communist/Socialist state.*
Neutral Nations	*Pro-Communist/Socialist Nations.*
Reforms -	*Programs that centralize controls and destroy Free Enterprise.*
Progressive -	*Any pro-Communist, pro-Socialist movement.*

When a Vladimir Putin, former head of the communist secret police, says with a big, fat smile, "I'm for peace and democracy," Americans say, "Why, he isn't so bad, he's for the same thing I am."

Nonsense! In their Aesopian language he has stated emphatically, "We're in a war. I'm for winning it and the final emergence of a one-world Communist State!"

Certain specific words are not only vehicles for transmitting information (when properly understood), but they are also triggers which evoke strong emotional reactions. As discussed in Chapter Three, emotions can be stored systematically within the mind. Stored emotions need words or graphic symbols to act as trigger mechanisms which release these stored feelings. Words can and do trigger certain non-thinking emotional reactions.

The communists build strong emotional feelings toward certain words. They then use these words as "scare symbols" to activate people in specified directions. Americans have strong emotional feelings toward certain American symbols, such as the word "Lincoln." The thought of Lincoln makes us think of honesty, integrity, fairness, love of country, strength, etc. In Chicago, many years ago, the communists set up a school on Communism and called it the "Lincoln School," using the emotional impact of Lincoln's name to their advantage.

The word "American" has wonderful connotations to us all. Communists understand this well. A fantastic percentage of their front organizations use the word "American" somewhere in the title.

The hard left also likes to build words into effective trigger weapons which bring about feelings of disgust. Extremism is one such word. Americans have an honest aversion toward political extremes, and rightly so. Our nation is founded on balanced, rational thought. Whenever organized opposition toward communism and socialism arises, the radical left and their buddies immediately try to falsely identify these organizations as "extreme," and if the propaganda is effective, they emotionally chase people away from these patriotic organizations. They also do this to individuals.

Many times Communists know that in the future they will be opposed on certain programs that they haven't as yet implemented. They will build slogans and trigger words in advance so that when the time comes people will react as desired.

For many years in this country the communists used the word "McCarthyite" with great effectiveness. They took this manufactured word and built fantastic negative emotions around it. In the creation of the scare word, they systematically destroyed Joe McCarthy the man.

McCarthyism still holds many sad memories for me. When I was in college, I was affected by the unfavorable propaganda relating to Senator McCarthy. I was anti-Communist, but I swallowed hook, line and sinker, the anti-McCarthy propaganda. It wasn't until years later and after much research on the subject that

I recognized the disservice I had done to this patriotic man. I still smart when I think about it.[10]

New "trigger words" are constantly being thrown into the mental American hopper, and many old ones constantly revived like ultra-conservative, extremists, neo-Fascists, and anti-Semite, just to name a few.

America is waking up!

One tactic that is a favorite of the Socialists is to take their strongest opposition, destroy or disgrace it, and thus all of the lesser opposing forces will readily fall. A good example of this today is the attempt to assassinate the character of the Tea Party people.

The hard leftists now seek to create a new scare word. This would evoke a conditioned response in a background of fear, founded on the specter of a Fascist plot inside the United States, which would attack all minorities, and spread terror to everyone. This left wing propaganda objective is a terror maneuver. It would be what they call the "correct" line for this time, to make the American public jittery through pressure from abroad, by manufactured crises in places such as Libya, North Korea, and the entire Middle East, and by pressure at home through visions of a "Fascist revival." A jittery United States citizenry would be off-balance, vulnerable and inactive.

The left is trying to make the "Tea" Party a scare word. People who are not aware of the tea party's independent structure and its membership might look upon it as a nutty group if they had no personal contact with the good folks in the organization and had no other source of information than the left leaning main stream media. The fact that a legitimate Pro-American organization **can** be downgraded, and such strong negative emotional reactions created within segments of the general public, is a clear guide to the past effectiveness of programmed negative emotions.

The leftist control of the main stream media is becoming more and more evident to the general public. The broad and open use of the internet, talk radio and Fox News is bringing attention to the leftist bias of the mainstream media. America is waking up.

Chapter Six

Analyze Your Audience

Charlie Conservative and Johnny Wright were deeply involved in a heated discussion. The subject matter was what some Americans refer to as, "The Babel on the East River," better known to the general population as the United Nations.

Putting it mildly, they were dissecting the glass menagerie, pane by pane. Johnny and Charlie were involved in a verbal game called ifs-man-ship or "If you think that's bad, have you heard this?" The object of the game is to assess all the bad news, add up all the "ifs," and then guess what year the socialists will take over the world.

Johnny and Charlie were having a grand old time. They were mildly disappointed when their conversation was dramatically interrupted when the New York cab in which they were riding pulled suddenly to the curb and abruptly stopped. Johnny and Charlie started to get out of the cab when they noticed that they weren't at their destination.

"Say Cabbie," said Charlie, "This isn't where we were going."

"This is as far as I'm taking you two nuts!" replied the irate driver. "This is my hack and I'd rather be caught dead than haul around a couple of squirrels like you. What-do-you want, **war**? What's-a-matter with you guys? Don't you want to talk to leaders from other countries? What are you—isolationists or somethin'? Ain't the wars we had enough for you—what-do-you want atomic bombs going off?"

Johnny and Charlie stood silently on the street corner, speechless. They watched the cab peel away from the curb and disappear around the first corner. The irate cabbie had even refused to accept their money. They were mortified.

Our two conservative friends had been graphically shown that they had another person involved in the ifs-man-ship game. The only problem was the cabbie didn't understand how the game was played.

Both were well-informed on the United Nations. They had been exposed to the pros and cons of this august body, and like most people who take the time to do an in-depth study, they recognized the glaring weaknesses of this organization and the enormous financial burden the U.N. is to the American taxpayer.

> We must decide what we hope to accomplish by our conversations.

Obviously, they hadn't taken the cabbie into consideration when they were discussing the iniquities of the U.N. Probably the only contact the cabbie had ever had with the U.N. was the New York Times. He hadn't read anything that opposed the U.N. and he obviously had been won over by United Nation propaganda.

Charlie and Johnny found out the hard way the effect their conversation had on the cab driver. They learned a lesson. What were their mistakes?

First, although riding in his cab, they were oblivious to the cab driver's presence. There were six ears in the cab not four.

Second, if they were aware that he was listening, they assumed he knew as much as they did about the U.N.

Third, they lost an opportunity to inform those who might be listening.

We must decide what we hope to accomplish by our conversations. What are we after? Are we trying to convince the person to whom we are speaking of something important? Are we trying to prove just one specific point? Are we trying to neutralize a liberal argument? Are we trying to sell a listening third party? What's our time element? Do we have the time to make our point? These are just a few factors that we should take into consideration when we address others.

Let's look at some of the factors to consider in planning a conversation.

The Time Element: Time is an important factor. One day I was introduced to a local merchant by a good friend. I had never met the man before. I could tell that he was emotionally disturbed and pre-occupied by something that had happened before we arrived. He was bursting at the seams to share his feelings with us, so I inquired: "What's wrong? Something seems to be bothering you."

"You bet something's bothering me. My stomach is a nervous wreck! I have just been subjected to the worst lunch I've ever had."

"Was the food bad?"

"Food! No! It was the company. Do you know what they said?"

Without waiting for my reply, he launched into a blow-by-blow account of his luncheon conversation.

"Why, those nuts I ate with told me that our government was infiltrated with left-wing socialists; our foreign aid works against our nation's best interests; we are becoming bankrupt and we're getting much closer to a major depression and the main stream media doesn't tell the truth. They believe that our educational system is subverted by the unions. They also said that the bureaucracy is trying to confiscate all our guns. Gad, what a couple of nuts. What do you think?"

"You're right," I replied, "They're nuts!"

This shopkeeper was a good man and obviously not too informed. He had been subjected to a couple of conservatives who tried to give him a two-year educational course in a twenty-minute lunch. They had not only alienated this man, but they may have created in him a long-lasting gastric disorder.

46

I would like to pose this question to the reader. Do you think they were effective conservatives? How difficult do you believe it will be for anyone to approach this shopkeeper on any of these subjects again?

The Time Element is very important! It is a common conservative mistake to oversell. We make good points and then proceed to destroy everything we say by over-saturating our audience. There is a saying among salesmen, "Sampson was a piker. He killed 1,000 men with the jawbone of an ass. Every day at least 10,000 sales are killed with the same weapon."

"Patience" should be one of our best weapons. Wyatt Earp, the famous frontier marshal, was once asked how he survived over one hundred gun fights without a scratch. His reply was, "I drew very slowly—but with haste."

Within that story is an object lesson for conservatives. Are we trying to neutralize a liberal? Our chance of converting all liberals is

> We must act—
> not react!
>
> We must be aware—
> not unaware!

nil, but if we can prevent them from using left-wing clichés, we have at least stopped them from transmitting harmful propaganda.

If you are capable of shooting down one of their pet clichés, you can be reasonably assured they won't use it again. Nobody (especially a Fuzzy) likes to have his old ego bent out of shape.

How many people do you know who love to argue for the sake of argument? These people generally are wonderful transmission belts for passing on conservative ideas. That is, if they are given a good point or two.

Some people argue **purely** for the sake of argument. They argue liberally to conservatives and conservatively to Liberals. If you have given them a good reasoned argument, you can bet that they will use it on the first liberal with whom they come in contact.

Be aware of your audience; understand what you are trying to communicate—then do it! The conservative who "draws slowly, but with haste" is tremendously effective. In other words act—don't react—be aware, not unaware.

Chapter Seven

A Liberal Look at Conservatives

Have you ever asked yourself, "What is a conservative? Or better still, why am I a conservative or even am I a conservative? Why do I think the way I do, react the way I react, or act the way I act?"

All of us who profess to wear the conservative garb should know some of the answers to these questions. I contend that not enough of us ask ourselves these questions often enough or try to answer them.

I make no claim to being a psychiatrist, psychoanalyst, doctor, witch doctor or crystal-ball-gazer. I leave that to the collectivist mentality. I can, however, through just good old-fashioned horsesense, much study and exposure to conservatives over an extended time, (not to mention I'm married to one), make a few observations on what makes us tick. Why is this knowledge important? It is vital because our mental make-up has a direct bearing upon how we discuss issues with our friends. Knowledge about ourselves and how we react to given situations and word stimuli can mean the difference between winning converts or chasing people farther into the collectivist camp.

You may be assured that the Socialist mentality and especially the communists are well aware of how we act or react under given conditions. They take advantage of our reactions at every opportunity, trying to use our energy to their advantage or channeling our energies into paths which will dissipate our effectiveness.

Well, what is a conservative?

I contend that the bulk of Americans are fundamentally conservative. Most Americans want to conserve our traditional American values, conserve our national honor and our nation's reputation, conserve our Nation's institutions, conserve their family ties and conserve our Christian ethics, and especially conserve our Constitutional freedoms.

This chapter is basically written for the informed or those who want to be informed and are an anti-big government American. I shall attempt to point out certain personality traits that we, as traditional conservatives enjoy. These characteristics are the basic ingredients of our nature and affect our actions and reactions. These fundamental beliefs are the corner-stones on which we base our actions.

> Knowledge about ourselves and how we react to given situations and word stimuli can mean the difference between winning converts or chasing people farther into the collectivist camp.

In the previous chapter we mentioned the word "conservative" and how people react to it. Now, let's talk about people who are conservative.

I'll start out making matters even more confusing by stating that we have different kinds of conservatives. I'll define two in particular. In many ways they are as alike as two peas in a pod, but in other ways they differ noticeably.

First, the traditional conservative: This person is what the name implies—a conservative. Let's call them Betty and Bart. Both are slow to act, they mull ideas over and over, exploring all ramifications before acting. Traditional conservatives are not gregarious, they usually have a few solid friends whom they treasure. They usually dislike large gatherings, and when given a chance will avoid them if the event is just a social gathering. However, when it comes to events affecting the nation's future, they show up no matter how large the gathering.

Bart and Betty dislike giving speeches or imposing their ideas on others. They like to be left alone and prefer leaving others alone. Once finding something that works for them, they adhere to it tenaciously. A traditional conservative has strong ethical beliefs—things are right or wrong, true or false, good or bad. In other words, to them there is not much gray but a lot of black and white. They look upon themselves as realists. You couldn't call Betty and Bart out-and-out blue sky optimists by any means, but it would be unfair to call either one a pessimist either. They could be both depending upon the circumstances, but still, more of the former than the latter. They are suspicious of public relations, people, actors, politicians, and extroverts in general. Both Betty and Bart are solid, bed-rock and dependable.

A Jeffersonian (wee bit libertarian) conservative is a horse of a slightly different color. Sherry and Sam are generally more optimistic. They have the ability to see the light side of everything. Both have a good a sense of humor and tend to be idealists. Their goals are always high and sometimes not too practical. Sam and Sherry like people, like crowds, both are gregarious and out-going. Sam would rather not, but if his principles are in question, will give a speech, Sherry will debate with strangers, Sam accepts leadership, and Sherry instigates action and programs.

Both are willing to take a chance because they believe optimism and hard work can carry it off. Both like new things and think contemporarily on material matters. Both like public relations and think that some of their fellow conservatives are sometimes too old-fashioned in how they approach the public.

Both Sherry and Sam are as sound as Betty and Bart in their basic principles and also have a deep sense of right and wrong. Quite often Jeffersonian conservatives and traditional conservatives clash

with each other on how certain programs will best be implemented.
They sometimes get mad at each
other and can't understand "why"
other conservatives would react a
certain way.

> We believe in an all-
> powerful God, His
> son Jesus Christ, and
> the Holy Spirit.

Let's now look into areas where
Jeffersonian conservatives or traditional conservatives are "like"
two peas in a pod.

Point I: *Both believe in the Almighty.* We believe in an all-powerful God, His son Jesus Christ, and the Holy Spirit. We believe that
He created the universe, the earth and us. Because He loves us like
a father, He has plainly established how we should behave upon this
earth. For our benefit, He has given us rules, laws, and a code of
morals to happily live by. He has established our relationship with
our fellow man and how we, as His creation, are expected to per-
form. God tells us in no uncertain terms to love His Son and obey
Him, or expect the consequences!

God has given us standards, and as believers we use these standards to evaluate ourselves, our neighbors, our nation, and the world.
We believe that evil is a separate and dominant force upon this earth,
whose sole function is to separate all of us from God.

We recognize that only God is all-powerful and all-knowing. We
believe that man is finite and has no right to play God with anybody.

Point II: *We are individualists.* We respect the integrity of other
individuals and expect this in return. We believe man controls his
social environment, not the other way around.

Point III: *We feel responsible for our own actions.* We usually
look to ourselves first when something goes wrong instead of finding
someone or something to blame.

Point IV: *We are self-supporting.* Generally we take care of
ourselves and our own, and expect others to do the same. We like
to help others when they ask for help, but would consider it both

rude and debasing to interject ourselves into their lives without their express desire. We vigorously resent others who attempt to play God and Godfather to those who don't want it.

Point V: *We respect authority.* We are taught from childhood to respect our parents, our teachers, our American institutions, our Constitution, and our church. We are impressed by those, who through study and self-sacrifice, gain positions of authority. We believe these positions of authority should be used honorably and with dignity.

> We dislike those who lie and look upon prevaricators as people of weak character.

Point VI: *Because of our moral standards, we evaluate what we hear, read, and study.* Based upon what knowledge we have, we then sift, assess and come to conclusions. People who come to conclusions rarely ask questions—they make statements, emphatic statements. I might repeat this because the "coming to conclusions and making statements" aspect of the conservative is of key significance. It affects his whole attitude in conversations.

Point VII: *We try to be truthful.* Usually we try to answer every question posed to us. When asked, we feel a compulsion to state our views. We are sometimes aware that what we believe may not be "popular," but we feel that if we don't answer, we are not being moral. Often we carry this too far.

We dislike those who lie and look upon prevaricators as people of weak character. We are not compatible with "professional politicians" who twist the truth glibly and bend it to fit a certain audience. They make us very apprehensive.

Point VIII: *We tend to be emphatic individuals.* Right's right and wrong's wrong. Black's black and white's white. We generally speak our piece in a few words (most often in the form of a statement). Diplomacy is not an art to which we conservative males pay much attention to. Our wives are far more blessed.

Point IX: *We are impatient.* A well-informed conservative finds himself doing a lot of things he would rather not do; like participating heavily in politics, attending meetings, giving speeches, and finding himself in a position of having to inform others on the nature of communism and socialism. The prime concern of a conservative is "let's get this country shaped up so I can get back to doing what I did before." He or she's in a hurry.

The idea that this is a long-range project isn't too appetizing to their conservative palate; in fact, it's downright distasteful. We tend to become extremely impatient with others who aren't doing their part. They are a constant source of frustration. "What's **wrong** with them? Can't they **see** what's going on?" we impatiently inquire.

Conservatives usually underestimate their own abilities and intelligence. They often ask: "If I am bright enough to see the problem, why can't others?"

Point X: *Conservatives tend to anger easily.* We might not always visibly show our anger, but you can often count on it being somewhere inside us. Why do we anger? Simple—when you combine our knowledge with our conclusions, add our strong sense of right and wrong, sprinkle in our impatience, and put us into a situation where we are conversing with an individual who thinks everything is "peaches and cream," you're going to have an angry conservative on your hands.

Point XI: *Sometimes we give the impression of being dogmatic, self-righteous, overbearing, and often develop the "either you're with me or you're against me" complex.* Because of our convictions, we frequently do seem overbearing; in other words, we sometimes come on like the wrath of God. Because of our impatience, we often appear dogmatic. We have a strong sense of individual and national morality; it is a vital factor to us. Generally we bring this into our conversations and sometimes, if we don't watch how we project our position, we may appear to be "holier than thou."

Christ was the only one who could say, "He who is not with me is against me" (Luke 11:23). When we develop this kind of attitude toward our less-informed friends (and we often do), we literally close the door to useful communications. People are "with us" by the intelligent way we inform.

Point XII: *We abhor all forms of totalitarianism.* We have a deep-seated distrust for those who carry the banner heralding the omnipotence of any form of government. We have faith in the individual because we believe society is formed of individuals. We believe in the uncommon American, and we believe they only become "common" when they grant divinity to demagogues.

We are **for** freedom—thus we must oppose any negative program which subverts free people. History has proven conclusively that the dictator can dictate only when he

> Power **does** corrupt
> and
> absolute power **does**
> corrupt absolutely!

has a centralized government to enforce his demands. Power **does** corrupt and absolute power **does** corrupt absolutely.

We become distraught when we see good people gravitating towards the siren call of centralized government. Our minds project to the inevitable conclusion of such folly and we shudder.

Point XIII: *We deem ourselves fortunate to have been exposed to such great minds as our forefathers such as Thomas Jefferson, Benjamin Franklin, Patrick Henry, James Madison; free enterprise economists such as Ludwig von Mises, Frederic Bastiat, F.A. Hayek, Henry Hazlitt; and modern authors such as William Bennett, Leonard Read and William Buckley.* The wisdom that these great men project offers the mind solid food in a sea of economic and political pabulum.

It is important to recognize that there are also different kinds of "sometime conservatives" who are hot buttoned only when their hot button bell is rung. For example, there are single issue fiscal conservatives who care little about social issues and social issue conservatives whose interest in monetary matters is of secondary importance.

It is very important in our fight with our common enemies, the collectivist mentality, to remember what we conservatives have in common and not get bogged down at election time internally picking nits when the pits are on the other side.

I believe just about all conservatives believe that in this complex world, the degree of freedom we now enjoy is directly the result of our forefather's deep understanding of Scripture and their ability to transfer such knowledge into a Republican form of Constitutional Government.[11]

> Knowledge is power. Ignorance is the pliable putty of the demagogue!

Knowledge is power. Ignorance is the pliable putty of the demagogue.

Chapter Eight

The Broad Brush

Be specific. Generalizations have a tendency to work against the people who use them. Conservatives get their dander up when a commentator refers to all conservatives as extremists. Liberals get their dander up when conservatives refer to all liberals as left-wing wackos. Both are justified in their complaints.

Let's skip the "broad brushing" that is used against us, and concentrate on **our** own misuse of generalizations. Let us analyze the negative effect it has upon our attempt to free Americans from the growth of bureaucracy.

As an example, we use the term "government" too loosely. "The government is leading us down the road to socialism. The government is giving aid to our enemies. The government is becoming totalitarian. The government is rotten to the core, etc., etc."

Most Americans look favorably upon the government because they believe the government is the will of the American people. We are raised to respect our form of government, enabled by the Constitution and the Bill of Rights. Americans consider the government to be an extension of the public will, and this is as it should be. However, Americans

> Generalizations have a tendency to work against the people who use them.

have taken our government for granted, and have forgotten that government, if not constantly restrained, can become the oppressor instead of the servant. So when we, as fellow Americans, knock the government, those who don't understand what we mean sometimes feel that we are knocking our country and them personally.

We conservatives want to conserve our constitutional system, and because we have taken the time to understand how it should work, are naturally appalled at how it is being perverted into a bulging, wasteful bureaucracy. It is not being perverted by the majority of people who work in government—just a dedicated, well placed socialist-minded few. Most of our government employees are faithful Americans, and when we use the "broad brush" we paint in many people who don't deserve it.

Be specific. Say, "There are those in **our** government who are trying to destroy it. A dedicated minority of Socialists and legislators have forced **our** government into the position that..." "Some are manipulating **our** government, trying to change it so that it will..."

When you say the government is aiding Socialists, and it happens the person to whom you are speaking voted for the present administration, you are in effect calling him pro-left-wing, insulting his patriotism, his good judgment, and putting him in the position of being anti-American.

He'd probably dislike socialism as much as you do if he understood it, but feels a loyalty to our governmental leaders and believes they know "what they are doing." You can be reasonably assured that he doesn't understand subversive tactics, and how a few well-placed hard core socialist conspirators can affect our national policy.

By being specific, you can inform him of these subversive tactics, communist methodology, Socialist planning, etc. As an example, point out to him how Harry Dexter White, as Undersecretary of the Treasury, was extremely instrumental in formulating monetary policies which hurt our government.[12] Show him the key position held by this identified communist fellow traveler before he was exposed. Do the same with Alger Hiss.[13] Ask him how effective **he** thinks these men were in advancing communist doctrine in this country. After a while, he will put two and two together without your doing the addition for him.

The broad brush alienates—being specific educates.

> The broad brush alienates—
> being specific educates.

The general American population has been conditioned to believe that we, as fellow Americans, are "against" everything. When we use the broad brush, we fit the picture the left-wing paints of us.

This broad brush also may be used indiscriminately against other American institutions such as:

"The Press doesn't give us the truth!"

"Educators are subverting our children."

"The colleges are left-leaning."

"The churches promote Socialism," etc.

These are generalities which "trigger" people to react against us. It's okay to say there are those in the main stream media who manipulate news and don't tell all the truth and then give an example to prove your point. Some educators subvert; specific college professors are left-leaning; and some church leaders do promote socialism, but not all. Again, be specific.

We are against any program that subverts our American institutions because we are for truth and freedom. Jefferson once stated, "Any fight against tyranny is a positive action."

Whenever we resort to "broad brushing," we hurt our cause and thus our nation.

Be factual, be specific!

Chapter Nine

EGAD! Here Comes Carrie Nation!

Deep down in my heart I feel a great deal of compassion for the newly awakened pro- American, anti-socialist, pro-constitutionalist citizen. When a normal, everyday, 24-carat American discovers that everything isn't "peaches and cream" and that our country is in deep, deep financial trouble, he or she goes through a truly traumatic experience—to say the least! He or she is really something to watch. In fact, you can almost predict the stages that someone will go through.

The first is "The Awakening." This stage is of short duration. Some good friend or casual acquaintance slips Charlie or Mary a piece of "light" reading, such as Senator Jim Demint's book "The

Great American Awakening" or Michelle Malkin's "Culture of Corruption" or Ann Coulter's "Demonic" or David Limbaugh's "Crime's Against Liberty."[14] Our good friend takes the book without much comment or even too much interest. They probably have received the reading material from a hard-core Tea Party friend, whom I like to refer to as "one of the fastest pamphlets in the West."

Our friend politely takes the book without even reading the title then drops it on a table, promptly forgetting about it. Later that evening, by chance, the local TV programming isn't up to par, so he picks up the material for a little educational light reading. Four hours later, his eyes dilating and breath coming in short gasps, it dawns upon him, "Gad, if this is true, we're in **deep** trouble!" That night is a restless one. The next day they seek out the friend who gave them the information, and asks him if he has anything that substantiates what they have just read.

"The fastest pamphlet in the West" always has a second book or pamphlet on hand, and the "newly awakened" can't wait until work is over so they can resume their reading. They polish off the second pamphlet or book by early evening. After another sleepless night, deep reflection, anguished thoughts, and typical American concern for their country, our friend comes to a decision: "I've got to do something about this!" So, attending their first Tea Party meeting, our good friend has discovered that socialism is evil personified and that they had been taken in by the main stream media! "Double Gadzooks! I better get busy!" Our friend is now in the second stage—a full fledged, wake up the world "Carrie Nation."

The next day, armed with copies of his newly acquired reading material, he descends upon his place of employment (or close friends), with all the aplomb of a Mack truck. He or she grabs the nearest person, waves the book or E-mail under his nose, and declares: "Wake up! We've got problems with the Socialists. **You've got to read this stuff!**" Our "Carrie Nation" is peddling bad news; out of character with what his friends have known him or her to be. A week ago he or she was happy-go-lucky and now he or she is "The Avenger."

An argument usually starts at this point.

"Well, old pal," asks his friend, "Where are all these left-wing

Socialists you're talking about?"

Our newly-informed Tea Party recruit is now two-books and one meeting wise, and suddenly finds himself confronted with arguments never encountered before.

After a brief bit of sputtering, our newly informed friend exclaims: "Good grief, man, they're **everywhere**."

His acquaintance who has been pre-conditioned against right-wing extremists ranting about Communists, Socialists and impending financial disaster, exclaims pitifully to himself, "Horrors, my pal's over the hill. He's flipped his trolley and become an extremist!"

Our newly-informed anti-Socialist patriot bashes his head into one stone wall after another, ricocheting from friend to friend. Nobody seems to listen as he uses the force-feed method of education, which consists of grabbing an acquaintance by the lapels and stating, "You've got to read this shocking stuff!"

The tragedy is that our newly-informed friend is right! We do have a problem. The material that they have been reading is correct and well documented. But "Carrie Nation" has run smack into the result of insidious conditioning of the American public to reject anti-communists, anti-socialists, and anti-bureaucracy citizens as extremists. Our newly informed patriot is unaware that what they analyze as apathy and lack of concern on the part of their friends is nothing more than the result of the conditioning process of years of bad information by the main stream media.

So our friend goes into a third stage—Depression saying things like, "It's too late. It's all over. Nobody cares."

At this point, they back off from trying to awaken people. "What's the use? They deserve slavery!" Melancholy sets in and whenever he hears the "Star-Spangled Banner," he gets a far-away look in his eyes. He also gets a bit cynical. He may say to himself, "You might go down the tubes, but not me." He starts to look around in Army Surplus Stores for camping gear and asks his wife to look into food that can be stored for a long time. They decide that this year, instead of spending their vacation at the beach, they'll camp out in the mountains or the local woods with the kiddies and get back to nature." Our friend starts doing exercises to get back into condition, avoiding fatty foods (bad for hiking) and even considers giving up smoking (bad for the lungs).

All this time the newly awakened American continues reading. He or she becomes more and more informed on the nature and tactics of the country's enemies. He reads everything he can lay his hands on; and finds others who feel the same way and slowly, but surely, matures into the fourth stage—"the knowledgeable, articulate pro-American conservative or Tea Party activist."

Our new conservative recognizes by this time how many pine cone nuts it takes to feed a growing boy. He recognizes that nothing can be gained by giving up and heading for the hills. He is cognizant by now that all of those with a vested interest in maintaining and expanding the governmental bureaucracy are directed by a dedicated, conspiratorial few whose cover is deceit, confusion, criminality and lies. He knows that those who want to change America into another Socialist welfare state **can** be defeated by a properly informed citizenry, and so he sets to work. He or she is, by this time, aware of the insidious conditioning process that has taken place on their good friends and neighbors, and so **intelligently** they start to inform effectively, get active and, I might add, win!

> **Intelligently,**
> they start
> to inform
> effectively,
> get active,
> and win!

Chapter Ten

Name Dropping

(Use Authorities)

Quite a few years ago, I was invited to give a lecture on "Communist Front Tactics" to a group of interested citizens in an adjoining city. One of the hostesses decided to invite a rather large group of people for a social hour before the lecture to meet us.

After a few formal introductions, I gravitated to the snack bar and located myself strategically near the creamed cheese dips. I struck up a conversation with another cheese-dip fancier and, while we merrily dunked potato chips into the rapidly disappearing delicacy, we argued on everything from soup to nuts. The only thing we agreed upon was the quality of the cheese dip. Before long, we had to leave for the lecture hall. My cheese-dip friend and I had a gay old time discussing the issues of the day.

As I walked out of the door, I could hear his wife saying to him,

"Dear, did you have a good time talking to the speaker for tonight?"

"Speaker!" was his shocked reply, "Do you mean I was arguing with the speaker?"

When I arrived at the hall, he was waiting for me, and I had no sooner gotten my foot out of the car than he started apologizing profusely. I was embarrassed. I just couldn't get it across to him that I had enjoyed arguing with him, and what difference did it make, anyway, if I was the speaker?

Later on it dawned on me. What I had said at the party as far as he was concerned was just one man's opinion, but when he found out that I was an **authority** on the subject, it made all the difference in the world.

The funny part about this whole thing is that this lecture was the first one I had ever given on that particular phase of Communism. I was roped into giving the talk because of the persuasiveness of a good friend. They needed a speaker that night and I was the pigeon. The club, with the help of good publicity, built me up as an expert so that they could turn out a good audience. I know **one** person who believed the advance propaganda.

The point is, from our earliest days we, as Americans, are taught to respect legitimate authorities; our teachers, our ministers, our officials. It is an integral part of our American fiber. The liberals know this. They are constantly creating "Authorities" out of thin air on this and that, so they can feed their propaganda to us through "reputable" sources. The communists set up "fronts" for this purpose, and always get a professor, minister, or "highly-rated" individuals to add authenticity and respect to their programs. The general public isn't aware of this devious tactic, and unquestioningly accepts these so-called authorities.

The conservative rarely takes advantage of an American's respect for authority. We must develop the ability to quote reliable authorities. A conservative will read a book such as Robert Morris' "No Wonder We Are Losing,"[15] and then proceed to expand on the facts offered to him in the book. He will come to conclusions and it

> Learn to use legitimate authorities in your conversations.

will usually appear in conversation in this manner:

"Sam, do you know that communists have been working in this country for a long time? Why, they were even in New York in 1940 manipulating the Teachers' unions!" (conservative statement).

The person to whom our conservative friend is trying to communicate could reasonably conclude, "Well, that's your opinion. So what?"

This same statement could have been worded more effectively in this manner!

"Sam, the other day I finished reading, "No Wonder We Are Losing," written by Judge Morris who, as you probably know, was former Chief Council for the Senate Internal Security Subcommittee. Judge Morris stated that in the State of New York, in 1940...."

Sam, at this time, has a hard time saying, "So what?" It has been presented as an authority's opinion—not yours. Sam is now in the position of arguing against Judge Robert Morris—not you.

This is what I mean by name-dropping. Learn to use legitimate authorities in your conversations. The hardest people to convince are all too often your closest friends and acquaintances. It is difficult for them to believe that you might know more about anything (especially about politics or communism) than they do, so when you try to convince

> Don't give the impression that "you're smarter and they're stupid."

them **you** know more, you are literally trying to be a prophet in your own country. Even the Lord Himself had that problem. Jesus stated it emphatically in Mark 6:3 and 4. Look it up.

A person could actually bring someone who knew less about the subject than you do, introduce him as an authority on the issue in question, and his "authority" would be believed before yours would. This is just human nature, the old ego at work again, that brings on this phenomenon.

Your chance of convincing somebody who doesn't know you too well is actually better than trying to convince a relative. Since a stranger doesn't know you, he is far more willing to accept you as an authority on a subject if you approach it properly and sound knowledgeable. Now this is the proper time for "name-dropping."

"The other day I attended a lecture by so-and-so and he stated. . . ."

"The last Congressional Budget Committee report on our national debt stated that in two years our grandchildren's debt would. . . ."

"William J Bennett as Director of the Office of National Drug Control Policy said about hallucinogenic drugs. . . ."

"Friedrich A Hayek, in his Nobel Prize winning book on Economics, offered this suggestion. . . ."

This establishes that you study and have reliable source material. In essence, it sets you up as a serious student of government. We have many outstanding authorities to quote—let's use them.

As a word of warning, don't give the impression that "you're smarter and they're stupid." No one appreciates a know-it-all. That's the first lesson in "How to Lose Friends." Don't ever fib—know your sources and present the facts properly.

Next time you find yourself in a discussion with friends about socialism or politics, drop the names of recognized authorities that you have read; such as Leonard Read, Fredric Bastiat, Hayek, David Limbaugh, and Orwell just to name a few. When you combine this with, "What do you think?" (a question), and then keep your friends on the subject, you will be much more effective than when just expressing your own opinion. As a good thought, when you read a good book or article, think how you can use the material and the expert's name when discussing the subject with a fuzzy friend. It might turn out to be fun.

Chapter Eleven

Conservative Astronauts

S everal decades ago, we launched men into space. The satellites raced around the world at an awesome speed, circling the globe within hours. People were impressed by these fine astronauts who literally established new horizons in man's limited knowledge of space travel.

In the exploration of the outer limits, we conservatives have overlooked the speed of travel of the "inner limits."

Let me give you an example: You and a Fuzzy friend are discussing the weather, children, and other friendly-type subjects. Everything is peaceful and harmonious. Suddenly that uncontrollable urge comes over you to get into a different area of conversation—our military boys fighting in Afghanistan. So, in typical conservative fashion, you say: "I read in the paper today that the President said nothing about winning that war. I think that's horrible leadership!" (a typical conservative statement).

Your friend responds, "Bush should have never gotten us into that expensive war in the first place. Don't you think that money would be better spent on food and education for the underprivileged in our major cities?" (a typical liberal cliché with question).

You respond with, "Oh, I think we spend more than enough on welfare right now, it's financially breaking our back!" (a conservative statement).

Your now-ignited friend replies, "Do you mean you go along with cutting funds for the elderly, for those who are poor and starving?" (a heated question). Etc., etc., etc., etc., and so forth.

You, my friend, have just become an official conservative astronaut! You have been taken from the war in Afghanistan to welfare in America in less than six seconds. Pretty fast travel, if you ask me!

> Most people don't like to arrive at new conclusions.

The important subject and the one you wanted to talk about was the war in Afghanistan! What in the world are you doing winding up discussing American welfare?

Your friend unconsciously changed the subject. His knowledge on Afghanistan was obviously inadequate or he would have continued with that subject matter. The fault at this point lies at your doorstep, **because you let him change the subject**.

Conservatives are constantly falling into this verbal orbit. **Keep your friends on the subject!**

If you allow them to take you from one subject to another, you will never get any of your points across because you are allowing them to use every cliché they have at their command. Inevitably, they will throw a barrage of questions at you until they get you into an area where you are not equipped to argue, and then they pounce upon you. Before you know it, you've been nailed to the wall. You will walk away with the distinct feeling that your friend thinks you are "Count Dracula" while he is the "Standard-bearer of Mankind."

I repeat, keep your fuzzy friend on the subject! This sometimes requires patience while they run through their verbal labyrinth. Sometimes it takes a polite interruption, but no matter how you do it, always come back to the original subject until you have completely exhausted your friend's knowledge on that particular matter. This can be done by ending everything you say with a relevant question.

When you keep your friend on the subject matter he has to think beyond his surface knowledge to compete in the conversation. When this happens, he isn't reacting as he has been conditioned to react and that is what you are after!

It is only when your friend mentally admits that he doesn't know much about that particular subject that he will possibly listen or admit that you have pertinent information that is important to him.

Most people don't like to arrive at new conclusions. Subconsciously, the old ego factor takes over, and will ruffle their tail feathers. When you see this happening, back

> Don't be a conservative astronaut and take those fanciful flights from one liberal cliché to another.

off a bit, compliment your friend's intelligence, and offer him a book to read on the subject you've been discussing.

Say something like, "Charlie, I know you are vitally interested in this subject. I have a book that would help fortify your knowledge on this matter and, besides that, I sure would appreciate your comments on this 'document'."

It is time to smile sweetly and remember an old adage, "More flies are caught with honey than with vinegar."

If you want to see a book snapped up in a hurry, try that approach. One thing you do want is your friend's opinion. If you have just pinned him on this particular subject, you can bet your bottom depreciated dollar he doesn't want to be boxed again. If you can get your friend to read, a big chunk of the battle is won.

Another point: Conservatives often bite on the tempting bait offered by a new channel of conversation. You probably know something about that subject too, so you easily follow along. That's another trap. At best, all you will be doing is matching tit-for-tat; liberal cliché for conservative cliché.

Conservatives also have the dandiest compulsion to answer every question that's asked of them, and while they are trying to think up answers, the Fuzzy is thinking up a new cliché to shove down their throat. A person can talk at a certain speed, but again, the mind works at about three times that speed. So, while you're talking (making statements), they're thinking up another cliché.

Next time, take a good look at the person with whom you are conversing. Nine times out of ten, he isn't really listening. He's waiting for you to shut up so he can pose another question.

The moral of this chapter is: "Don't be a conservative astronaut and take those fanciful flights from one liberal cliché to another. Find your subject and stick to it!"

Chapter Twelve

A Conservative Look at Some "Liberals"

We sometimes have a tendency to classify as liberals all those who disagree politically with us. I believe that this term is too broad to be descriptive. I dislike categorizing people, but unfortunately folks, by their actions and thoughts, have a tendency to categorize themselves. Ideas do have consequences. For the sake of clarity, it is necessary to discuss a few of the ideological slots that I believe Americans fall into.

Let's talk about the biggest segment of the American population, the lovable "Fuzzy."

"Fuzzies"

A "Fuzzy" is your friend and mine. He may be a next-door neighbor whom you like, a bridge partner of long standing, a golf buddy, a business acquaintance, a close relative, or a nice guy. A Fuzzy is a person who loves to talk to you about everything, except religion and politics. When perchance you do broach these subjects, he will unknowingly parrot left-wing clichés. He is a person who never has taken the time to notice the contradictions in the mainstream media, the ideas of his leftist friends, his political party, or his own fundamental beliefs. He has accepted certain leftist dogmas, believing full well that they are his own ideas.

A Fuzzy says he loves his country and its Constitution although he knows little about the history of America or the substance of the Constitution and the Bill of Rights. The problem is that he doesn't understand how these founding documents have been subtly altered or ignored by the political left, nor does he want to admit that anyone would want to corrupt these institutions or could possibly succeed in doing so. He takes great comfort in the belief that, "It can't happen here."

A Fuzzy resents your trying to awaken him to the realities of life. He is prone to accept any argument that seems to diminish the conservative position, including the occasional time-worn left-wing tactic of name-calling. Our Fuzzy friends like to think of themselves as rational, sensible political moderates, therefore any other opinion contrary to their own tends to border on the extreme whether left or right.

They dutifully vote in every election for **all** the candidates of their parent's party. They often state that they, "Vote for the man, not the party," but they seldom do. They base their opinion all too frequently on opinion polls, their local left-wing newspaper report or editorial, which they believe to be honest, objective reporting. Or, some out-spoken "friend," often a union buddy, who usually knows less than they do.

Our Fuzzy friends distrust all politicians and often refer to politics as "too dirty" to get into. But for some strange reason by the plurality of an election vote, they believe the candidate is suddenly sanctified and cleansed by the elective process and, by osmosis acquires a dedication to "the people."

If the Fuzzy is a businessman, he usually is ethical, hard-working, and conscientious. He generally runs his business conservatively, gripes about his taxes, but meekly pays them thinking they help the poor. He's a good father, good companion, and a sports fan. He's "disturbed" but not too worried over the nation's trillions of dollar debt, but believes that "those guys" in Washington (whoever they are) will take care of it.

In fact, outspoken conservative friends, talk radio and Fox News usually make our Fuzzy friend nervous. He dislikes what you and they say because it sounds too frightening to be true, so he listens to the alphabets: ABC, CBS, NBC & CNN. If cornered, he will avoid what he calls "political conversation" because, being basically a good person and if he accepts what you say he will **have** to do something about it.

So before you can finish your first sentence, he interrupts and pleasantly says, "There are two things friends shouldn't talk about, religion and politics."

If our Fuzzy is a woman, she is often active in some community project; she's a good mother and wife, and doesn't have time for all those "deep" subjects with which you seem to be so intensely preoccupied.

"Oh," she probably will say, "Let's talk about something that is more pleasant; I leave **those** matters up to my husband." Her husband, unfortunately, is generally as fuzzy as she.

Every so often one of our dear Fuzzy friends stumbles across the cold, hard facts, and realizes maybe his or her conservative or tea party friend wasn't so kooky after all, or he finds somebody who says we are kooky. At that moment of truth, he begins to study and dig into the responsibilities of American citizenship or conveniently forgets it. Often though, he too is loudly denouncing socialism, big bureaucratic government, and other political diseases which infect our nation.

We should all have great compassion and understanding for our Fuzzy friends, and do what we can to expose them to the truth. Instead of getting mad at them, we should realize that, "There but for the grace of the Almighty go I."

"China Eggs"

My grandmother used to have a number of porcelain china eggs around the farm. They were used to encourage the hens in the coop to lay eggs. Grandma would put several of these eggs in a nest and, before long, some hen would settle herself on the eggs and try to hatch them. I guess these porcelain beauties brought out the mother instinct in the barnyard cluckers, because they would sit for days on top of these phony eggs, clucking away, trying to hatch them. All they would accomplish was to warm them up a bit. As soon as the hen would leave the nest, the china eggs would cool off.

> Some people just don't **want** to wake up to what's happening to America!

I contend that today a sizeable number of Conservatives are wasting their time perching on top of china eggs, trying to hatch them into full-fledged fighting eagles. In other words, we all have a few friends to whom we have been feeding material for years, trying to stimulate them into taking an active interest in what's going on. All that we accomplish is to warm them up while we are "perched" upon them. As soon as we leave them alone, they revert to their clammy, cool, porcelain nature. Some people just don't **want** to wake up to what's happening to America. In fact, some people just don't seem to care.

If we ever get our country moving in the right direction again, our china egg friends will be the first to say, "See, I told you there wasn't anything to worry about!" or "We could have done it better our way."

I have a china egg friend. In fact, I think old Charlie is a classic example of Porcelaina Americana. I worked on Charlie for almost a year until I finally recognized the porcelain veneer with which old Charlie was coated. I'll bet I handed him at least thirty pounds of books to read. I'm positive that they are resting, unread, in some dark attic corner of Charlie's house, far out of Charlie's sight, and especially out of sight of any visitor that Charlie might have. ("Can't be too controversial, you know.")

Charlie frustrated me for almost one full year. I even contemplated a unique plan that I thought might awaken him. Late one night I mentally envisioned this approach. I'll scare the be-daylights out of him!

Charlie is a creature of habit. He goes to work every morning at 7:55 a.m. and arrives home punctually at 5:42 p.m. He plays bridge every Thursday night, and waters his lawn every Sunday morning at ten. He wears the same garb every Sunday for his pilgrimage to the crab grass—thongs, a beat-up sweatshirt, frayed shorts, and a baseball cap. Charlie's weight has shifted over the past twenty years, and he sort of looks like a relaxed pear, held up by a pair of toothpicks.

My plan was to have a truck race up to my house (which is directly across the street from Charlie's), at 10:05 a.m. on a chosen Sunday morning. The truck would have the United Nations police force symbol attached to the side. In the truck would be several of my friends dressed in U.N. garb even with blue helmets perched upon their heads. The truck would screech to a halt; the troops would leap from the truck, smash in my door, enter and drag me screaming, from the house. Charlie, I knew, would stand there stupefied, taking it all in.

At a strategic moment, I would break away, dash madly across the street screaming loudly, "I told you so, Charlie! Save me!"

I would then throw myself to the ground at Charlie's knees, hold his legs transfixed so he couldn't move, while my U.N. buddies took pot shots at me, the escaping prisoner. I can mentally picture Charlie now, spraying water everywhere as he desperately tries to disengage himself from my vise-like grip upon his skinny, shaking legs.

After chuckling to myself, I immediately dismissed the thought. It might have worked, but I doubt it. After Charlie found out it was a hoax, he would then be convinced beyond all reasonable doubt that his neighbor across the street was the nut he'd always thought he was.

At this point, I hope that no one misunderstands me, because I like Charlie; basically he is a good guy. Like many others, there is something in Charlie's make-up that makes him oblivious to the issues of the day.

The point I want to make is that we have to evaluate some of our friends. If they are "china eggs," don't waste valuable time on them. There are plenty of people who are ready to take an active part in the fight to save our Constitutional Republic, and stop our plunge into governmental fiscal insanity. There are good folks out there who are willing to join the fight if they are properly approached.

It is often comfortable to approach "china eggs." They rarely argue with you; they usually nod their heads in agreement. Besides, if by some strange fate you "hatched" one of your china egg friends, he would probably be a chicken anyway.

The American Liberal

I differentiate a contemporary American Liberal from a Socialist. The latter I don't care much for, the former I sometimes like. Before my contemporary conservative friends start a movement to drum me out of the lodge, let me define the differences.

Liberal-lites

Many nice people in America today consider themselves "moderates" or "Liberals." They sometimes work and support leftist leaning candidates. Many are active in some organization in which the conservatives wouldn't be caught dead—like the democrat party. They usually are democrats because of family loyalty; their parents and their grandparents were democrats. They have scant knowledge how dramatic the political parties, especially the democrats, have changed in the last thirty years.

Some are businessmen who have been conned into helping some new environmental cause, trying to save some endangered flea or a threatened buzzard. Some have lent their name to an organization which promotes the equality of man, through government planning and control of everybody. They think it's good for business!

Most of these later day liberals are bright. While in college, they listened to their left-wing professors and were tilted to the port side of the political boat. They honestly look upon themselves as contemporary thinkers who believe they have a unique understanding of what's happening at home and abroad. They look upon us (conservatives) as being old-fashioned, narrow-minded, and to some degree, reactionary. Much to the chagrin of conservatives, they are glib of tongue, forceful and articulate, and seem to have an ability to constantly put most newly informed conservatives in a defensive position in a political discussion.

Deep down inside, they are still Americans who have an aversion to excessive governments, but they believe that our government's bureaucracy isn't one of them. They believe that we, as Americans, should be subservient to our government, and that "our" bureaucracy is a proper vehicle to promote all good things. They talk about government, but as a group, are unaware of how it really works or how deeply enmeshed our nation is in debt. They have accepted all of the information from the major media as objective news and view the New York Times as the epitome of truth.

They have been so indoctrinated into "Liberalist Mentalis" that to question their present views and admit they could be wrong would severely shake them. They have a vested emotional interest in liberalism. Admitting to themselves that they have promoted harmful programs is unthinkable.

It is a common, and I might add an incorrect assumption, that these liberal-lites don't read and are uninformed. The fact is they do read, but unfortunately what they have read or heard has been in a variety of Marxist social gospel and what they haven't read much of is American history. Many liberals follow the line of the Mecca of media, the New York Times or the Washington Post. If so, they have been led to believe in global warming, the endangered spotted owl, and think one world socialist government might be a good thing and that the real threat to America is the Tea Party.

> Old myths die slowly, but die they do!

The mainstream media has pre-conditioned them against conservative publications, conservative books, talk radio, and blogs. When more factual material did permeate the American scene via talk radio, the internet and a wealth of conservative writers, these lefty-lites, believed they were listening to science fiction.

Some conservatives might disagree with me, but I am firmly convinced that if this country ever gets close to a real state of totalitarianism, a sizable segment of these Lib-lites are still Americans.

They might see the light and come out fighting—better late than never! Some of the radicals of the sixties got married, had kids, had to get jobs and pay taxes and now find the love affair of the left and going a week without a bath has lost its charm. The bright ones became aware that science has discovered how massively complex Darwin's simple cell really happens to be! Old myths die slowly but die they do.

Viewing America's present predicament and the future of their kids, many lib-lites are taking off their rose colored shades to see red, white and blue. Those who do will be welcome.

Socialists and Communists

Socialists and communists are liberals of a different color. They have rightfully been called watermelons, green on the outside and red inside. Both are intellectual aberrations and contradictions bereft of common logic. As an example, both promote centralized powerful government, shouting to the sky their love of equality and help for the underprivileged. In the same breath, they spew forth venomous propaganda against free men and women and the free enterprise system who happens to be the great creator of jobs and wealth for the so called "underprivileged" that they say they support. Socialists of all stripes are godless and to be pitied. The only difference between the two is that communists, who happen to be more organized and deadlier than their socialist comrades, when given control will murder all who effectively oppose them. Socialists are more humane, they bore men to death with their platitudes and officious control. Both are proud atheists. We must pray for them to come to their senses because what eternity holds for both of them is unthinkable, we wouldn't want that for even our worst political enemies.

A friendly word of advice to all atheists, "If close to death, swab yourselves with suntan oil because where you are going you'll need it."

Chapter Thirteen

Humor

Humor, I sometimes believe, is becoming a lost art. A good old-fashioned belly laugh relaxes the bones and lets the sunshine through. It also helps you keep your perspective.

Poking fun at a particular set of dogmatic beliefs is an age-old American custom. Modern liberals, in their attempt to be serious, are sometimes down-right hilarious and, at times, so are some conservatives who become so wrapped up in the seriousness of the problems facing our Nation that they lose sight of the power of humor, not to mention its medicinal effects.

A good conservative friend of mine came charging up to me one day waving a newspaper article with mayhem in his eyes.

"Bill, did you read this? Get a load of this propaganda! Have you ever seen such outright lies? Read it—go ahead—just read it!"

By this time I had the distinct feeling he wanted me to read the article, so taking the paper from his shaking hand, I started to read.

It was written by one of the local starry-eyed socialists of sophomoric sentimentality. The writer in question was typical of the self-anointed saviors of humanity. In about fifty per cent of the article he carries the torch for the brotherhood of man and the fatherhood of government. In the other fifty per cent, he condemns those whom he considers anti-brotherhood. In other words, anyone who dares to take a position to the right of that paragon of truth and question the virtue of Barack Obama is a nut cake.

The article dealt with the "paranoia" of the radical right (unnamed but implied), the manic-depressive tendencies of said groups, and the inability of these people to grasp the complexities of this enlightened world. It was angry and frothy to the point of being a bit hysterical. The author ended his vitriolic assault upon the conservative community by stating that calmness, love and reason should prevail. He showed little "love" in his article. This struck me as being hilariously funny, and so I did what came naturally, I laughed. My conservative friend didn't get the point.

"What's so blankety-blank funny?"

I pointed out the glaring contradiction in the article and why I considered it so humorous. After a moment of consideration, my friend stated, "You know, that article is a bit ridiculous." Then he chuckled a bit also.

A few days later I again met my buddy. He had a big smile all over his conservative countenance and was in a visibly rare mood. The contrast from our last encounter was startling.

"Why the big grin, Sam?" I asked.

"Well, Bill, you know that article I showed you? I had shown it to several people before I saw you and wound up in a few hot debates. I guess I was mad because I hadn't gotten anywhere with these people. After I left you, I showed the article to some more people and pointed out its incongruous aspects,

> We should recognize that humor is a powerful tool.

and I'll be darned if they all didn't see the ridiculous nature and the humorous contradictions. You know, Bill, maybe we should all laugh a bit more at these comics."

I agree! I don't think we should slap our sides in merriment every time a left-wing pundit opens his mouth, but we should recognize that humor is a powerful tool and the left-wingers are constantly dropping big **faux pas** into our laps, which we can use to point out the ridiculousness of their position. The left-wing establishment constantly pokes fun at the average American—we should poke a bit in return. If you want to see ultra-southpaws ignite like a roman candle, poke a little fun at their pet dogmas and their glaring contradictions.

Analogies

Through humor you have a wonderful vehicle to inform your friends. Unfortunately, people remember humorous situations a lot longer than they remember cold, hard facts.

As an example, one friend of mine when discussing the United Nations uses a very effective and humorous analogy. He asks:

"What would you think if law enforcement sat down with the moon-shiners to discuss

> Americans are optimists who love a good laugh.

crime and law enforcement. Then, after they all gathered together, the good guys and the bad guys, law enforcement stated, "Some of your people are up in the hills making booze— let's go up there and get them!" And then the moon-shiners looked up, smiled, and vetoed."

Simply stated—that's the U.N. where our dedicated enemies have veto power. People will remember that simple analogy.

Talk radio host Rush Limbaugh is a masterful story-teller who ties humorous situations to present-day conditions. Because of this ability, he has millions of daily listeners who repeat his words of wisdom. With wisdom and humor, he drives the left nuts. Some of the analogies Rush uses are classic and should be repeated time and time again.

The next time you hear a good joke, anecdote or analogy, remember it and use it. You will be surprised how some jokes that at first don't seem to relate to the conservative humorous weapon system can be modified to work.

An acquaintance reminded me of a wonderful old analogy that Abraham Lincoln used to prove a point, which is easily applied to today. It is extremely contemporary if properly used.

Mr. Lincoln asked his friend, "If you call the tail of a dog a leg, how many legs would a dog have?"

His friend answered, "Five, of course!"

"No," said Lincoln, "You can call the tail of a dog a leg, but that doesn't make it one,"

My friend uses the same analogy, and then he relates the joke to certain RINO Republicans. "Isn't it true you can call so-and-so a Republican, but does that make him one?"

A liberal professor was demonstrating to his students how some trained fleas responded to verbal commands. "Jump," he shouted, and the fleas jumped. He then reached down and picked up one of the fleas and with a pair of tweezers, removed its legs. He placed the flea back upon the table and once again shouted, "Jump!" Of course, the poor flea could not. "Observe carefully students," smugly stated the liberal professor, "once you remove the legs from the flea, it becomes deaf."

Left wing politicians like the professor are continuously coming to the wrong conclusions, even when inundated with irrefutable facts. One could conclude that somewhere in their cranium there is a loose screw flopping around, or they have some other agenda that they would rather not talk about.

There is an old expression, "Nobody likes a sour mouth." Did you ever ask yourself, "Do I come on like the wrath of an enraged bull when I approach my friends? Does my concern for my country so encompass me that I lose my perspective and become overly emotional when I talk about big government and Socialism? Have I lost my ability to laugh at situations and myself?"

If that's the case, you have to ask yourself, "Am I really helping the Tea Party movement?"

Never in our country's history has so much depended upon

rational thought. Emotional love of country is a wonderful thing, but if we are incapable of controlling our emotions and others control us, our job of communicating is all the more difficult.

Ask yourself, "Have I ever won anybody to my point of view when I was mad?"

A sense of humor definitely relaxes everyone. A joke in good taste keeps a friendly conversation going. Our job is to convince people there is a serious problem and jar them into taking an active role in solving it. Humor can help if you use it properly and it will help you feel better at the same time. Remember, sour-mouths usually don't win. Americans are optimists who love a good laugh.

Chapter Fourteen

The Common Denominator
or
Ox Goring

A few years ago while I was lecturing to a group about the evils of socialism, it was obvious that I had a sympathetic audience—they remained awake; that is, with the exception of one kind soul. His head kept falling forward, and I am sure he would have started snoring if it hadn't been for his wife's sharp elbow constantly jabbing into his side.

Surely he was attending under duress. He obviously didn't care much for what I was saying, or else he didn't understand. It could have been a little of both.

Later, I changed my tactics and started commenting on taxes. I quoted one fact about how many taxes were in a single loaf of bread, and suddenly my sleepy friend snapped to attention and hung breathlessly upon my every word.

Somehow I had "gored his ox."

Later, after the audience had departed, I asked the hostess, "Who was that fellow in the corner?"

"Oh," she replied, "he's my next door neighbor. His wife's okay, but he's been a tough one to talk to."

"I really got to him on the loaf of bread taxes."

"No doubt," she said, "he's got eight kids and the local bakery truck is by his house twice a day."

With that gentleman I had found a "common denominator." We both disliked hidden taxes, especially when they are wrapped in cellophane.

The way to find the common denominator is through questioning the person to whom you're speaking. Sometimes conservatives try to cover a multitude of subjects, seeking to find something that will interest the other person. This can more often work against you than for you, because, if not handled properly, you can wind up in a heated debate long before you stumble across something on which you can both agree.

Probe. Ask questions. Ask their advice or opinion. Try not to commit yourself until you find a common denominator.

How often have you heard a fellow conservative bending some uninformed housewife's ear on the fiscal irresponsibility of the Federal Reserve System's monetary policy? The poor lady couldn't even contemplate, much less discuss intelligently, the fiscal irresponsibility of the monetary system because she has little time to understand the subject.

> Try not to commit yourself until you find a common denominator.

Talk to her about her five children's education. Ask her about Johnnie's, Mary's, Suzie's, Henry's and Tiffany's education, or lack thereof, and you probably will have a tuned-in audience.

Each person has to relate to the subject matter. We sometimes get so "fact and figure" conscious that we overlook the necessity of matching our message to our audience.

50,000,000 deaths by communist hands is a statistic; a child killed by a car on your block is a tragedy. The truth is they are both tragedies. You can talk about the many American deaths in Afghanistan and that is a statistic, but if you say that twenty-one-year old Sergeant Smith lost both legs due to a landmine planted by the Taliban, and, note that he could have been the next-door neighbor's boy, that congers up thoughts that mean something.

The better you develop the ability to paint verbal pictures which people can see and identify, the better you communicate. Your ability to emotionally involve a person in the conversation has a great deal to do with whether he or she retains what is said.

Remember, emotions play a large part in getting a person active in the anti-Socialist fight. Emotional involvement is not a sin. Righteous indignation is proper and just. Anger however, can be harmful when it clouds reason.

I get emotionally upset when I think of the crimes being perpetrated against humanity by any totalitarian system. I would be less than human if I didn't. But if I allowed my emotions to rule me, I would lose my ability to reasonably approach others.

It is characteristic of conservatives to build their emotions upon facts while liberals build their "facts" upon emotions.

Our national bureaucracy has become so large that Americans have a difficult time personally relating to it or understanding its machinations. Last years billions are today's trillions. Millions, billions, or trillions, for that matter, are just statistics which people have become accustomed to hearing about.

> The better you develop the ability to paint verbal pictures which people can see and identify, the better you communicate!

The conservative says, "We're trillions and trillions of dollars in debt."

"So what?" thinks his Fuzzy friend to himself. "I'm living fine. I've heard that gripe before. That's just conservative propaganda."

It is obvious that your Fuzzy friend has no idea how the national debt relates to him and what it will mean to his children and his grandchildren's children. If he did, he wouldn't say, "So what?"

Ask your friend, if he might go shopping, buy something worth thousands of dollars for his personal use and charge it to his children's account, knowing full well that they would be expected to pay if off when they came of age?

No thinking parent would do that intentionally. Then point out and ask, "Isn't this exactly what we are doing by allowing the government to go deeper into debt, knowing that this generation won't pay it off?"

Our task is to do a better job of relating our subjects to our friends so they will understand. When you graphically show people how much one trillion seconds happens to be then translate seconds into dollars, maybe your friend will see how much in hock their kids and grandkids are already in—fifteen trillion dollars of national debt! Maybe then, "trillion" might mean something terrifying to them.

A million seconds is 12 days,

a billion seconds is 32 two years,

a trillion seconds is about 32,000 years.

Find out how you "gore" the interest of your friend. Sometimes (pardon the pun), all you have to do is "ox" him.

Chapter Fifteen

Know Your Subjects

It goes without saying that you should know something about a subject before you start talking. If you are not informed on a particular matter, at least you can keep people wondering about your knowledge if you keep quiet. Unfortunately, all too often people open their mouths and remove all doubt.

However, many conservatives believe they should know all about every facet of socialism and communism before they speak up against it. They feel they should know all the ins-and-outs as well as all facts and figures on free enterprise before they defend it. These people are not quite right because it is impossible for anyone to know **all** the facts. (This might come as a shock to some political southpaws, but it is true).

One thing anybody can do, by hard work and study, is understand the fundamentals.

If a person comprehends the basic function of law, knows the precepts of a free market economy, grasps the meaning of a Constitutional "balance of power" system of government, and then has studied enough of socialism to recognize its fallacies, he can hold his own in almost any political conversation.[16]

If he grasps the techniques the hard left employs, understands how they think, recognizes their tactics, and comprehends the conspiratorial nature of the lying left, he will find that he can handle himself quite well in conversations pertaining to this world cancer.[17]

It is common for folks to say, "I know all about these things, but I just can't talk about them." I say to you—baloney! If you really know your subject, you can talk about it. I'll prove it to you. First, you ladies, "Do you find it difficult to talk about your children?" I doubt it. In fact, if given the opportunity (if you're anything like my wife), you will go on for hours about their good habits, future, school, etc. You can talk about your children because you **know** them.

> One thing anybody can do, by hard work and study, is understand the fundamentals!

Now you gentlemen, I'll bet you could talk for hours about your business, favorite sport, your children's future, etc. You **know** and like the subject, that's why you can converse on the matter.

You can know and talk about politics the same way, **if** you take time to study and know your subject. But there's a difference between studying a subject and knowing it!

Knowledge is good only as it is applied. The socialists and communists, as an example, couldn't care less how much you study them, just as long as you don't take your knowledge and do anything with it. I know quite a few people who "study" communism religiously. If the communist/socialist cabal ever takes this country, these students will know exactly how it was done—big deal!

That is small comfort to them, or to you and me. I say again, "Use your knowledge. What good is it if it isn't applied?"

First of all, let's remember what we read. Unfortunately, the older we get the sloppier our reading habits tend to become. We subconsciously have a tendency to read for the emotional effect we receive from the book or an article. We seldom consciously read stuff to retain and pass on the information.

How many times have you finished reading a book, and when asked, "How was it?"

you replied, "It was great!"

"What did it say?"

"It said we were in awful trouble!"

"What trouble?"

"Oh, lots of trouble!"

"Where are we having this trouble?"

"Everywhere!"

"How come?"

"Don't ask me, read it for yourself!"

The person in question had read emotionally, not retentively.

How many times have you heard a good lecturer speak for two hours, and afterwards find you can't remember or repeat five minutes of what the speaker said? If this is the case, my friend, you read or listen emotionally.

It wasn't always this way. When you were in school you remembered what you read. You made a habit of remembering. Why? Because there was always some teacher around who had a habit of giving tests. We sometimes lose good habits that we have developed. Remembering subject matter is one of them. It is a habit that we have to develop again if we hope to convince others of the soundness of our position.

There are several techniques that are valuable reading tools. They will help you immeasurably if you use them.

The first technique is paper strips. This is a personal favorite. Take fairly large strips of paper and insert one every third page. When you come to the strip of

> Knowledge
> is good
> **only** as it is applied!

paper, close the book and try to conscientiously remember what you have just read. Probably you will be surprised how seldom you even remember the last paragraph. Then skim over what you have just read and watch it all come back to you. Then ask yourself, "How can I use that information in a conversation?" Then quietly verbalize it in practice, even if you happen to speak to a wall. There will be no applause, but if you do this, you will be pleasantly surprised at how much you might retain.

It is better to read one book well and retain its message than to read ten books and be unable to communicate on any of them. A book can be a wonderful tool. Between its covers, the author shares years of accumulated knowledge, hoping that it will benefit you.

The second technique is the old underlining with the pencil or marking pen technique. Sometimes we use different colored pencils or pens; red for real hot stuff, pale blue for secondary information, yellow for other paragraphs that you want to remember. I believe research books should be extensively marked. We're not in the fight to impress people with how clean and pretty our material looks on a bookshelf.

> It is better to read one book well and retain its message than to read ten books and be unable to communicate on any of them!

The third technique is to read the same book three times. I find that going back over books I have read before is tremendously beneficial. I learn and retain almost three times the information the second time around. If you have several books on the same general subject, read them all at least once and then be sure to repeat reading the most informative. This will give you a deeper insight, and enable you to derive even more benefit from subsequent readings.

Now, the fourth technique is to form a discussion group with friends on books, and write a short, simple outline on each chapter. This technique is a beauty. You share your knowledge with others and in return gain knowledge from them. Talking about a book and writing a simple outline implants knowledge firmly in your mind.

Fifth is to do you have a computer? If so, transfer to the computer stats and quotes you deem valuable and useable. I started doing this years ago and boy, am I glad I did! I have loads of good stuff to use now.

Since I write a little, these facts and quotes come in handy to emphasize important points of interest. Also, the transfer from book to computer helps my memory retain facts and makes it easy to transfer from computer to whatever I'm writing. I'll give you an example. Here is a quote from Robert E. Lee that I've used quite often.

> *"The truth is this: The March of Providence is so slow and our desires so impatient; the work of prog- ress is so immense and our means of aiding it so feeble; the life of humanity is so long and that of the individual so brief, that we often see only the ebb of the advancing wave and are discouraged. It is his- tory that teaches us hope."*

Isn't that a great quote? Knowledge of American history gives me great hope. We Americans are a special people, the progeny of generations of freedom loving giants. Let us never forget it.

There are many other valuable techniques which help. It isn't important what method you choose, as long as you retain and then use the material you read.

If you have sloppy reading habits, correct them. All it takes is reforming an old habit that you used to have. A habit, by the way, that's important to you, your country and to your children.

Chapter Sixteen

Like People

S everal years ago I attended a local political fund raising feed. All of the party-faithful were on hand to support this noble cause, and raise a few dollars for the local partisan hero. Many fine women worked their fingers to the bone preparing these soirees, hoping to secure a few dollars for their favorite candidate. The candidate usually gets the money and the attention while the unsung heroines of the kitchen get the leftover salad.

The gastric attacks that are suffered for the cause of Conservatism magnify during an election year. There are invitations to dinners, luaus, brunches, lunches, teas, cocktail parties, coffee hours, snacks, and every imaginable kind of assault upon the digestive system. If, perchance, the hostess does prepare some epicurean delight, the desert is usually a Pepto-Bismol speech that always accompanies this kind of gathering.

One of these days some smart politician will send out a letter stating that he is inviting you to a fund-raising feed-fest, but instead of insisting that you attend, he will offer you an alternate plan. He will send you a program of the events, the names of the guests of honor, a typed copy of the speaker's address and a letter which simply states that after paying the caterer, renting the dining hall, the speakers fee, all he will make on a fifty dollar dinner ticket is about twenty dollars per head, so why not send a check for twenty five dollars for you and your wife, then you and he will both be money ahead. It might work.

A particular backyard fund-raising function sticks in mind because of one small but significant incident. A few college kids were present who happened to be friends of the host's daughter. They were not conservatively oriented by any means. During the speeches, I kept glancing their way to watch their reactions. I could tell by their facial expressions that they were rejecting every other word. In fact, they thought our speaker was quite laughable. As soon as

> Antagonism toward an individual will show through and he will hear little of what you are saying!

the talk was over, I made a beeline to them.

I wanted to find out why they reacted the way they did. It didn't take me too long to find the ringleader of the group. After I introduced myself and asked a question or two, the young man who was sporting a sparse beatnik-type beard launched into a typical left-wing diatribe against conservatives.

After nearly one hour of patient discussion, I began to penetrate his left-wing clichés and start him thinking. The diatribe stopped, and he and his friends proceeded to ask legitimate questions. It was an hour well spent. They were good kids who, unfortunately, had never been properly exposed to conservative philosophy, and they seemed sincerely interested and intrigued.

In the audience I spotted a well-known politician whom they all knew by reputation. He is a gentle, considerate person, and I knew that the young men would be impressed by him, so I steered him through the crowd and introduced them at the first opportunity. The bushy-chinned youth brashly threw him a very pointed question.

He smiled, but before he could reply, a person sitting at the same table belched out venomously, "You damned beatniks, you've got a nerve asking a question like that!"

I wanted to strangle the loud mouth right on the spot. The kid turned on his heel and marched through the crowd, visibly hurt, muttering, "Why did that guy have to attack me? All I did was ask a question. I'll tell you what's wrong with conservatives, they're name-callers, narrow-minded, etc., etc."

One complete hour shot. In fact, instead of any net gain, this youth was driven deeper into the liberal camp by an unthinking reaction from an angry "conservative" who should have known better.

We all should know better. It is easy to get mad, but anger is an emotion which gains nothing, especially when it is directed at the individual to whom you are speaking.

Aren't we Americans taught from childhood to respect another person's thoughts even though we disagree with him? Aren't they also one of God's creations? One may dislike another's ideas intensely and you may dislike socialism with a feeling bordering on passion, but if you translate that feeling into a personal dislike, you have completely shut off any lines of communication. Antagonism toward an individual will show through and he will hear little of what you are saying. Hating anyone is a weapon of our enemies. It is an all-consuming belief to them. Lenin taught hate. Hate big business, free enterprise, America, ownership of property, and hate God. Lenin preached it, taught it and believed that it was just another tool used to bring about world Communism.

Understanding, compassion, empathy, and concern for the well-being of others are vital parts of our American religious heritage. They are some of our most important tools. Resentment of an individual will cause a definite negative reaction to your conservative position. Result—net loss. There is a better way. Let's go to the Master for advice. In Scripture, Saint Paul in his second letter to Timothy gave this advice.

> *Avoid foolish and ignorant disputes knowing that they generate strife. And a servant of the Lord must not quarrel but be gentle to all, able to teach, patient,*

*in humility correcting those who are in opposition,
if God perhaps will grant them repentance, so that
they may know the truth, and they may come to their
senses and escape the snare of the devil, having been
taken captive by him to do his will. (2 Timothy 2:23)*

Isn't that great advice? If you are a conservative who blows off and gets mad at the slightest provocation, then you have two choices. One is to control your temper and look for the inevitable contradictions in their philosophy, and then as St. Paul advises, "gently correct them." Develop an understanding of people's mental mistakes and question the logic of their ideas. Or two, do the conservative cause a big favor by **please** keeping your mouth tightly closed.

Chapter Seventeen

The Greatest Weapon

Many years ago, when I first ran for public office, I was asked to speak before a local service club. It wasn't a typical speaking engagement—it was special. A few weeks prior to this talk, my political opponent, who was a liberal state assemblyman, had spoken to my service club. Now under duress, his service club was returning the favor.

The meeting was held above a bar, in a dark, poorly ventilated room. The atmosphere left a great deal to be desired; in fact, it was gruesome. It was obvious that they had strong pre-conceived ideas on what kind of a person I was. In their minds, I was "their boy's" opponent.

The audience was sparse; many of the members had stayed

home—so I thought. I was to speak on "Captive Nations." I had prepared my notes well in advance, and they were tucked in my inside coat pocket, getting damp from nervous perspiration.

I don't care how many talks a speaker has given, a hostile audience can and does make him very nervous. This time I wasn't just nervous, I was **extremely** nervous.

As is the custom, I occupied a seat at the head table. Someone placed the food in front of me, and I commenced to eat. I dislike eating before I speak, but I wasn't going to tip anybody off that I was ill-at-ease; and not eating is an obvious clue to a nervous stomach.

I looked up from my plate and tried to observe the audience—what there was of it. I had the feeling of impending doom when one of them would look at me with a, "I know something you don't know" grin, and then look away.

The time for my talk drew near. My mouth had that dry-cotton feeling; my palms were wet with sweat. My nervousness, in a matter of moments, turned into raw fright, for just as I was about to be introduced, a hoard of people entered the room, filling it to overflowing! They were laughing and joking with my opponent who was with them! They were all there for the hanging—**mine.**

My opponent had a chair reserved for him directly in front of the podium. It was all pre-arranged. The goose was about to be cooked, and my opponent was there to watch the plucking.

I wish I could say that my eyes filled with excitement at the challenge that had been presented to me, and that like James Bond 007, I picked up the gauntlet that had been thrown upon the podium, and with complete confidence faced the dawn, firing squad, et al.

But what I would have liked to have been, and what I was, were two different things. I was no longer nervous—I **was**

> We have, if we ask for it, the greatest of all strength, the help of the Eternal God!

petrified! My mind was numb. Instead of just having cotton in my mouth, I had the entire cotton belt. I felt that white fluffy stuff was coming out of my ears. My shirt was wet from perspiration—I was a mess!

I heard the club program chairman introduce me and, with no

small effort, I stood up and moved toward the podium. This wasn't **just** a speech. It wasn't **just** a political campaign. My opponent and I were as opposite as night and day. This campaign was to me a moral as well as a political battle. It was serious business.

The distance from my chair to the podium was a little over six feet, the length of a grave. **I bowed my head and prayed.** I asked God for help and asked Him to use me. I took my damp notes out of my pocket and discarded them upon the table. I grabbed the podium in both hands, looked out over the grinning audience without the foggiest idea of what I was about to say. My eyes slowly viewed the crowd, finally resting upon my opponent.

I spoke and was startled by the fact that my voice was sharp and clear, "I see that my opponent is here, and I believe that this is to the advantage of the audience. Instead of just hearing me, why don't both of us present our views on matters that concern you—the voters?"

My opponent was startled. He hadn't expected this. He tried to decline, but I forced the issue. Finally, he moved around the podium and faced the audience, which was an equally unprepared for this as he.

The first question from the floor was about the Captive Nations— the debate began.

For one complete hour I could do no wrong and he could do no right. He got mad, lost his composure, ranted, and raved. He went down in flames in front of his own audience—hoisted by his own petard!

It was a great day!

After it was over, my administrative assistant and I descended the stairway and walked out into the sunshine.

He turned to me and said, "Bill, I think God was with you today."

He was right. How did I know? Simple, **I didn't have either the nerve or the mental agility to handle myself as well as I did. I don't have that kind of strength. I asked for and received help. I felt a confidence and strength that I had never known before.**

Ever since that day, before every speech, I ask for His help and ask Him to use me. I never feel alone when I am on a platform.

We have, if we ask for it, the greatest of all strength, the help of the Eternal God.

After all of the study that you and I might do, we usually come to the crux of the matter. It is the fight between good and evil; the power of the Archangel Lucifer against our Savior Christ.

When we face this Satanic force, we are kidding ourselves if we believe we can lick it alone. We all sin, we all need a greater ally, and we have one. **He's there to help.** All we have to do is ask for the help of the Holy Ghost. All He asks of us is to follow Jesus.

It is important that we all avail ourselves of God's strength. We do that by constant exposure to His word, through the Bible and daily prayer. The best tool of all in bringing people to the truth is by our own personal witness. Let the Eternal Triune God work through you.

We have the greatest weapon! We who believe in God have the ultimate victory!

Appendix I

Man or Machine?

Have you ever looked upon yourself as an accident of nature? In other words, have you ever given much thought to whether you were created by a supreme intelligence (God), or that you owe your present existence to a multitude of accidents in nature which took thousands and thousands of years to complete?

Man has and should ponder his origin. Who am I? How did I get here? Where am I going? How should I live? Man usually comes to one of two basic conclusions. There is a God and He did create the universe and all that is therein, or two, there is no God and thus man is nothing but a graduate animal, developed over millions of years through a total evolutionary process, and now owes his existence to accidents which took place within nature.

Our whole Western civilization is built upon the first premise, that man is a created being; he has a Creator, and this Creator has established moral laws as well as physical laws, which determine how mankind shall live together.

There are those who accept the premise that man is nothing more than a graduate animal, but in his everyday life, he still lives by the rules and regulations of a Christian civilization. We are at this time not concerned too much about this kind of atheist.

We should, however, be very concerned about the International Communist Movement and their one-world buddies, the Socialists. They believe that man is just another animal, however a very complex beast. They believe that there are smart animals (that's them), and there are dumb animals (that's us). The Communists believe that we, the dumb animals who accept a divine Creator, are idol-worshipping slobs.

Lenin, the daddy Communist of them all, wrote that, "Atheism is an integral part of Marxism. Consequently a class-conscious Marxist party must carry on propaganda in favor of atheism." Lenin also stated that, "Religion teaches those who toil in poverty all their lives to be resigned and patient in this world, and consoles them with the hope of reward in heaven. As for those who live upon the labour of others, religion teaches them to be charitable in earthly life, thus providing a cheap justification for their whole exploiting existence and selling them at a reasonable price tickets to heavenly bliss. Religion is the opium of the people.* Religion is a kind of spiritual intoxicant, in which the slaves of capital drown their humanity and their desires for some sort of decent human existence."[18]

[*This aphorism was employed by Marx in his criticism of Hegel's Philosophy of Law. After the October Revolution it was engraved in the walls of the former City Hall in Moscow, opposite the famous shrine of the Iberian Virgin Mother. This shrine has now been removed.]

If a person took the time, he could fill a volume with all the quotes that Socialists and Communists have made attacking all forms of religion. From these morsels of blasphemy, you probably get the idea, if you didn't already know it, that Communists are dyed-in-the-wool atheists. In fact, to be a Communist you **have** to be an atheist—it's fundamental!

I might add, atheists are not necessarily Communists. In fact, a few atheists are strongly anti-Communist and anti-Socialist, but you can bet that all Communists are atheists. If they weren't they wouldn't be allowed in the movement. .

Now we have to ask ourselves, "What does this mean to us?" We know that Communists are atheists. We know they don't believe in God—so what?

Their attitudes mean a great deal to us because their very thoughts and attitude towards God, or lack of God, dictates their actions. From their viewpoint, man is nothing more than a very complex animal, comparable to an extremely complex machine that walks, talks, and sometimes thinks. His opinions, beliefs, and attitudes are totally brought about by the forces of society that surround him, i.e. what he hears, sees, or feels.

The Communists view man's brain as an intricate system of nerve wiring and memory cells, a circulatory mechanism which could be compared to a highly developed computer. Since man's brain, which directs his actions, is like a computer, it will respond like a computer if scientifically manipulated.

Much of their propaganda warfare is based on this concept. A computer cannot emit any information that hasn't first been scheduled (programmed) into it. A computer can only give data based upon what has been scheduled into its memory cells. Push a button and out comes specific information. Trigger the machine and answers are given based upon pre-programmed information. Such computers are a form of servo-mechanism. "Servo" means "slave" or slave mechanism. The scientific community has developed these slave mechanisms to speed up our productive forces, and today we have many computers which make business more efficient and effective.

Programming one of these machines is all-important. If incorrect information is fed to (programmed in) and stored in the machine's memory cells, naturally any "conclusions" of the machine are erroneous. The people in the computer industry have a name for it, "GIGO," meaning garbage in, garbage out.

The Communist looks upon man as a slave mechanism. Like his computer counterpart, he is to be studied and information is to be stored (programmed) in him, in the same manner as you would program a computer.

The conspiracy is doing just that and quite effectively I might add. The Communists believe that it is the State's function to control the programming of its subjects. They, the Communists, believe that man can be programmed to like or dislike, hate or love, be passive or violent. In a word, man can be made a "servo" for the State, and what's more, like it.

The London Times, May 16, 1956, reported on how the Chinese Reds molded the mind of a small Chinese businessman, and made him like it.

"....he saw which way things were going and he went along to the authorities to present them with his concern. Instead of thanking him for his generous and forward-looking offer, they chastised him pretty severely, told him that they were not at all satisfied that his offer was made of his own spontaneous will without ulterior motives, and sent him back to think it quietly over by himself. They would not interfere, they said; they wanted only willing and convinced volunteers. Back he went at the end of the month; back he was sent again to search his heart. Then, when he naturally pressed his offer still more fervently with each delay, and when they finally agreed that his motives were pure, they reminded him of his shareholders. Were they all of one heart and voice? He had to call a meeting of the group, and only then–when they were all clamoring to be allowed to tread the new way–only then did the state agree to take over the concern from them, promising them a share in the profits."[19]

It is interesting today in America how many businessmen are clamoring to get the government subsidies, contracts, advice and help, and how the state is promising them a share in the profits.

Back to China and the London Times article, "It was a glimpse into the process of 'moral regeneration or brainwashing,' about which so much is heard in China. It cannot be left out in any attempt to understand the forces at work...nothing is more striking than the skill and patience with which party members all down the line work on people's minds. Supported by all the social pressures, they spend hours, days and weeks in striving for conversion and willing cooperation wherever possible. And they get results, whether in public confession or private avowals. Where Russia set out to shape lives first and foremost, China is embarked on the task of shaping minds as well."[20]

In this grand plan for man, the Communists have a growing problem. They call it the counter-revolutionary mentality — that's us.

Because we are not "enlightened" to the make-up of man, and for some archaic reasons believe man is much more than a product of his environment, we stand as an ever-present danger to the grand new order. We are diseased people as far as they are concerned. We are infecting the world with our counter-revolutionary thinking. We offer to the world conflicting propaganda. So obviously we must be cut out of the world's political body like a surgeon would remove a cancer.

Individuals, groups, and whole nations **can** and **are** being programmed by Communist propaganda to accept dogmas which are alien to their own survival.

It is possible that by both omission and commission, a substantial percentage of Americans are being fed **controlled** information so that they react almost upon command. "Cybernetics" and "servo-mechanisms" are important sciences when used by those who wish to control the world. They are sciences of which we must be aware. People can be conditioned or programmed. Information can be conditioned or programmed. Information can be stored within an individual by design. People do act upon or react to specific stored information. Social environment, to a degree does affect man's outlook. He is affected by the information forces that surround him. **Many times like a computer, man will react in a pre-determined manner based upon his prior conditioning or programming.**

To believe that man can be totally controlled and to deny that man cannot, of his own accord, rise above or control his thought processes, is fallacious, but at the same time to deny that man cannot be scientifically programmed to think in a specific direction for a period of time is also incorrect. Abe Lincoln said it when he stated, "You can fool all of the people some of the time, some of the people all of the time, but you can't fool all the people all of the time."

By this time you are probably wondering what all of this has to do with winning arguments with your friends. It is vital!

We, because of our nature, background and moral training, are generally very predictable in any given argument. The Socialists and Communists have recognized our habits, and have systematically conditioned people to react against us and our arguments. Through conditioning, they have made black white, and truth falsehood; they have made individualism look selfish, and have tried to portray Conservatism as a dirty word. With their ability to influence communications, they have tried to pre-condition people to reject us as the bad guys.

As an example, the American people have been sold a big bill of goods on the United Nations being the greatest thing since sliced bread, but the Communists haven't stopped with just pointing out what they consider to be the most salable points of their "Babel by the East River." They knew that in time Americans would start questioning the effectiveness of this "instrument of peace." They started systematically to discredit through name-calling, innuendo and outright lies, all who might oppose the U.N. The portrayed the U.N. as above reproach and the anti-U.N.'ers as being intellectual infidels. So if you speak out against the U.N. in the expected manner, you identify yourself as an extremist and warmonger in the minds of many people.

The Communists have pre-conditioned people against an intelligent reaction to the U.N. Does this mean that you can't argue against the U.N.? Not at all, in fact, knowledge of pre-conditioning gives you an extremely valuable weapon in winning arguments. This was covered in the discussion concerning techniques of persuasion.

If you don't believe in this pre-conditioning, just go out tomorrow and strike up a conversation with a not-too-informed-friend. State that you think the U.N. is a Communist hot-bed, and watch him react against you. Then go to another friend (it is pre-supposed that you still have friends), do the same thing, and watch the identical reaction.

"What's-a-matter, do you want war or something? Don't you wanna talk with other nations? What would you put in its place, wise-guy?" etc., etc.

A conscientious parent doesn't wait until smallpox strikes his child before he does something about it. Wise parents take their children to a doctor and have them inoculated against the disease.

Communists, believing that we are diseased, are constantly inoculating people against our beliefs and principles. International Communism is still a serious and dangerous threat to America. The Reagan administration set them back but didn't defeat or stifle their desire for world dominion—**or change their minds**! They are stronger now than ever and we are weaker.

In past years, both houses of Congress had committees that investigated communist subversive activities and published reports for our citizenry, the Un-American Activities Committee of the lower house and the Senate Internal Subcommittee. The communists hated both committees and set up front activities to discredit and abolish both. They succeeded in doing so.

The California Senate had a committee on Subversive activities. I was an active member of that valuable Committee that reported on Communist activity in California. In the early 1970's, the liberal democrats took over the Senate leadership and the committee was no more.

Due to the election of left-wing legislators and continual propaganda generated by communist front groups, both Congressional Committees were disbanded over thirty years ago by the democrat control of Congress.

I know of no committee of either house that now investigates or reports to the public on communist subversion in America. The FBI under the direction of J. Edger Hoover actively investigated communist activities. Hoover's book "Masters of Deceit" is a classic on communists which all informed American's should read. Hoover served with great respect, honor and distinction under nine U.S. Presidents.

There has been a sustained effort by the socialist/communist movement to penetrate and influence all media. Serious students of communism understand this. How many communist cadres are in key media spots today? We don't know but we know that it exists. Whittaker Chambers, stated in his book "Witness" published in 1952, "There is probably no important magazine or newspaper in the country that is not Communist-penetrated to some degree" (page 475). This disturbing observation was made over sixty years ago.

Unfortunately today, our elected national and state governmental bodies pay small attention to subversive activities for fear of being labeled McCarthy-ites or witch-hunters by the national left-wing media. Speak out against big socialist government and be called an extremist. Stick up for constitutional rights and be treated like you're mentally unbalanced.

How could such a minority of left wing extremists gain such power when most Americans were raised to think differently? It's called patient gradualism and not understanding how our foes think and operate. They understand leverage and how to influence the public by impacting and influencing key areas of communication, education and government. Read more about it in the next Appendix.

Appendix II

Unnatural Reactions

If you had a violent fellow in your block that disliked you intensely and made no bones about it, I doubt if you would invite him over to your house to baby-sit your children. If this same fellow wrote a book stating clearly that he was going to kill you and your friends, and adding insult to injury, graphically outlined how he was going to do it with your money, you would probably think he was a candidate for the happy farm, straight jacket and all. But, if you loaned him the money then stood idly by as he proceeded to systematically carry out his detailed program of shortening your natural life span, you should be proper fodder for a psychiatrist's couch.

Freedom's enemies have written volumes of material on how

and why they intend to destroy our nation, and we don't seem to pay any attention. Simply put, we are their "good neighbor Uncle Sam" lending our loot and playing political footsie with "Ivan the Terrible and Muslim the Miserable."

It is not natural for any individual or nation to lend the enemy money, buy them arms and feed them, and at the same time disarm. I say again—it's unnatural.

How many of you have conscientiously planned long-range insurance programs to protect you in your old age, send your children through college, or protect your family from harm? How is it that Americans can look into the future in this manner, but at the same time be totally oblivious to totalitarian forces which are intent on destroying all of our future plans?

You don't build a new wing on your home when the garage is on fire!

Pavlov, in his experiments with animals (and later with people) discovered that the dogs could be conditioned to act unnaturally. A dog normally doesn't salivate when he sees an empty bowl of food. Man normally does not disarm himself in the face of an ever-present danger.

The radical Muslims, communists and socialists are systematically trying to condition the American people to act unnaturally. Through the use of emotional tensions, threat of war and nuclear holocaust, offering peace, racial riots, etc. America's enemies bring stress down upon the emotions of the people. If this stress can be applied repeatedly, deep anxieties can be generated.

Dr. William Sargant, author of "Battle for the Mind," stated: "Once a state of hysteria has been induced in men or dogs by mounting stresses which the brain can no longer tolerate, protective inhibition is likely to supervene. This will disturb the individual's ordinary conditioned behavior patterns. In human beings, states of greatly increased suggestibility are also found; and so are their opposites, namely, states in which the patient is deaf to all suggestions, however sensible."[21]

In other words, confuse people, create anxieties, and then when they are in a state of mental turmoil, suggest to them solutions which on the surface sound plausible, but underneath are totally opposite to normal behavior patterns.

Professor Sargant, commenting on the English people's susceptibility to propaganda during the Second World War said, "...hysteria was also evidenced in the susceptibility to rumors of Londoners during the blitz. Brain exhaustion led them to believe stories about 'Lord Haw-Haw's' broadcasts from Germany which they would have at once rejected as untrue when in a more relaxed and less exhausted state. The anxiety engendered by the fall of France, the Battle of Britain, and the blitz created a state in which large groups of persons were temporarily conditioned to accept new and strange beliefs without criticism."[22]

The fall of Cuba, only ninety miles away from our shores; South Vietnam, where close to fifty thousand American soldiers died; student riots; race demonstrations, and so forth, literally bring about in Americans the anxiety and confusion necessary to make them receptive to controlled programmed suggestions which are contrary to their basic nature. As an example, we sent aid to Communist countries while Americans died from Communist bullets in South Vietnam. If that isn't unnatural, I would like to know what is.

You may wonder what this has to do with talking to your friends about world problems. It has everything to do with it. The more aware you are of how people are affected by systematic conditioning processes, the more effective you will be in communicating. This knowledge allows you to better understand your friends. The whole leftist conspiracy is competing for people's minds, so the more you know of the enemy's tactics, the better equipped you are.

If you are aware of how your friends will react under given circumstances, you have a definite advantage in conversations.

By now you might be saying: "That might be true for others, but no one could brainwash me. That just doesn't happen to good 'ole normal Americans like me."

May I quote from Professor Sargant again: "It is a popular fallacy that the average person is more likely to resist modern brainwashing techniques than the abnormal. If the ordinary human brain had not possessed a special capacity of adaptation to an ever-changing environment—building up ever-changing conditioned reflexes and patterns of responses, and submitting for the time being when further resistance seemed useless – mankind would never have survived to become the dominant mammal."[23]

Professor Sargant then goes on to say: "That among the readiest victims of brainwashing are the simple, healthy extrovert."

Aldous Huxley spoke of the effect of mass conditioning in a special appendix to his, "devils of Loudun." He stated:

> *New and previously un-dreamed-of devices for exciting mobs have been invented. There is the radio, which has enormously extended the range of the demagogue's raucous yelling. There is the loud-speaker, amplifying and indefinitely reduplicating the heady music of class hatred and militant nationalism. There is the camera (of which it was once naively said that 'it cannot lie') and its off-spring, the movies and television.... Assemble a mob of men and women previously conditioned by a daily reading of newspapers; treat them to amplified band music, bright lights, and the oratory of a demagogue who (as demagogues always are) is simultaneously the exploiter and the victim of herd intoxication, and in next to no time you can reduce them to a state of almost mindless sub humanity. Never before have so few been in a position to make fools, maniacs or criminals of so many.*

Obama, anyone?

Dr. Sargant in "Battle For The Mind" states:

> *Despite the success of such assaults on the emotions, Western democracies underestimate their political importance. . . .It is still considered a mystery how Hitler persuaded even many intelligent people in Germany to regard him as little short of a god; yet Hitler never concealed his methods, which included deliberately producing such phenomena by organized excitement and mass hypnotism, and even*

*boasted how easy it was to impose 'the lie of genius'
on his victims.*

Hitler and Himmler were pikers in comparison with the International Communist movement in techniques of propaganda. They were the kindergarten variety compared to the Communists.

Normal people can be receptive to propaganda. If any of our readers believe that they can't be influenced or duped at one time or another by cleverly planned propaganda, then they are fooling nobody but themselves.

Appendix III

Majorities Elect? Hardly!
Connecting the Dots

Studying the mechanics of American politics, one soon recognizes that, on the average, only fifty percent of all adult Americans bother to register to vote. **Only half!** Then, in the primary elections, where the two major parties choose their candidates, again, **only half** of those who took the time to register to vote even bothered to participate in the primaries. So, only **one out of every four** Americans vote in primary elections where candidates for the general election are selected. It's quite a shock to realize that three out of every four Americans have no say-so in the selection of who the party candidate will be!

That's not all! Add to those facts, multiple candidates run in primary elections. It is not uncommon for a flock of eager political birds to show up wishing to nest in public office, some are vultures, a few are parrots and occasionally an American eagle. Each party chooses just one candidate; the number increases, especially when no incumbent is running for re-election or, when every ten years, new seats are created by reapportionment and the office is considered an "open seat."

Therefore, a small organized percentage of voters could nominate and elect their candidate in primary elections. The following is an actual example of how a small minority did win a major California

State Senate office. The registration favored the Republican Party.

District population approximately	600,000
Those who **could** register to vote	400,000
Those who **did** bother to register	235,000
Total of both parties who voted in the primary election	120,000
Republican party primary vote	70,000
Democrat party primary vote	50,000

Eight candidates, one conservative and seven others sought the Republican nomination. The conservative candidate gained just 16,000 of the total 70,000 republican votes and won! The other seven Republican candidates split the remaining 54,000. The Republican who came in second was 6,000 votes behind the winner and the newspapers announced the victorious conservative had won by a landslide!

The conservative Republican won handily in the general election in November. As the incumbent, he easily maintained the senate seat and served for twenty-two years. Using his office as an activist legislator, he gained leadership and helped elect many others of like mind.

Is this race an exception? No! It happens all the time. **Realize the significance of only 16,000 votes out of potentially 400,000 who could have participated. Is it any wonder that a small dedicated minority of activists could have a disproportionate impact on our government when so many Americans don't even register or bother to take part in primary elections in the very important process of selecting who their candidates might be? Think long and hard about "majorities" electing! Organized minorities elect!**

The conservative winner had a solid group of loyal conservative activists helping him—troops that manned the precincts, handing out literature, driving voters to the polls, strong minded conservatives willing to do the "grunt" work that it takes to win primary elections. They didn't sit around talking to each other, they realized that pounding the pavement and that an active minority who cares and works gets results. If moral people don't participate, just guess who does?

The hard left understood this numbers game many, many years ago. While Americans slept, a hard working minority has taken over the unions then the Democrat party structure and are now influencing our government. They did it from the grass roots up!

This is why the Tea Party activists panic the Democrat leadership and why the left are slobbering vitriol over this grass roots movement.

The left, especially the hard core socialists, saw that in local elections for union leadership, school boards, city council, supervisory races, an even much smaller percentage of votes could affect the outcome. With an organized minority of fellow activists, left wing candidates could, and have won many local offices. Once elected, and establishing a base of operations as an incumbent office holder, they found it easier to develop important name identity therefore making it much easier to move up, step by step, to higher office, such as state representatives and state senators. Then, at a later opportunity, on to Congress and the US Senate. Many a national left-wing Congressman and Senator have successfully followed this upward path and are now in national office, **and why not**? With patient gradualism, they've been at it for close to one hundred years. The results are obvious, in the US Congress of 2011, 83 of the Democrat Congressmen are members of the radical left "Progressive Caucus."

Once elected, even to the smallest seat, the socialist becomes an active part of the movement; committed to help promote left-wing socialist causes, and helping to hire on the public payroll others of like mind. They effectively use their offices to train staff, raise funds and gradually introduce, bit by bit, socialist legislation. For years and years, the capable activist moves upwards to one higher office after another—that is, if he or she remains a good socialist soldier.

The hard left socialists, in Democrat or Republican garb, believe that any method that achieves power is "ethical." "The end justifies the means" is their motto and method of operation. Deception and lying are the tools of their trade. To call someone a lying socialist is a redundancy.

During the early1900s, the "progressives" within the Democrat party were still too tiny to elect their numbers to many offices; they needed to attract additional support. Clothed as liberals, they increased their numbers by wooing and infiltrating small disgruntled and politically isolated segments of the population, offering them promises of future political advantage for their special and often extreme interests. Knowing that by adding small segments their combined numbers could add up enough votes to win primary elections. They first successfully wooed some segments of the union movement and later, through planned infiltration, they became a commanding factor in today's union leadership. Then over the years, adding little groups one at a time, they captured support from the homosexual community by sympathizing with their "gay" activities. They attracted anti-war pacifists, disgruntled feminists, extreme environmentalists, and any other dissident group that could be wooed with future promises of legislative support and jobs. Adopting Marxist "class action" agitation, they pandered to any group they could exploit and bring on board.

During the growth of their move towards power within the Democrat party, the leftwing leadership wisely kept these dissident segments in the background, separated and undercover, appealing to each special interest directly, and then, only to each one's special interest. They knew there would be difficulties if they ever brought them all together, for they certainly didn't want to have large meetings of rank and file teamster union members with the "gay" community nor the elderly with anti-war activists. They were especially clever in keeping these new "friends" out of sight of the old line Democrat membership.

The great depression of the 1930's brought the Democrats into national power at all levels of government, including active segments of the "leftwing hardcore." The majority of the democrat legislators elected during the 1930s and 1940s were still traditional Americans in their ethics and values. However, a few old-line Democrats saw trouble brewing and the shift in leadership taking place within their own party. The old timers found out later, when they found themselves, discouraged, gerrymandered out and replaced by a young leftist.

Over many years, the "extreme leftist" control over the inner workings of the Democrat party structure increased dramatically. Working together and directing these organized minorities during the nineteen fifties and sixties, the leftists had elected sufficient numbers to take control of the "Democratic" leadership of the large industrialized states in the 1970s and '80s. Thereby having the ability to select and elect more of their own to the legislature.

Being an organized and tightly controlled minority, it wasn't too difficult for the more radical element to gain positions of leadership within the majority party, thereby controlling the selection of key committee chairmanships. Again, it was a minority controlling the majority.

While in political office during the 1970s and 1980s, I saw the left grasp control over the political fortunes of the California Democrat party. On a first hand basis, I sadly watched it all happen as traditional American Democrats were eased out of office and out of leadership. Today, the radical socialists, although still a numerical minority, are the dominant voice in elected leadership, especially in heavily populated states. They effectively and systematically eliminated conservative Democrat office holders within their ranks. Because the Left now controls leadership, they control candidate funding, thereby dominating those who wish to be elected and effectively leveraging all Democrat incumbents to the left, especially those who wish to stay in office.

The socialists, over the decades, have developed an effective political farm system. They, like major league baseball, have a farm system of local left-wing politicians, governmental workers, legislative staffers, and Democrat consultants who they can count on to run for any vacated office. The upper echelon controls the money and effectively picks who moves up the ladder.

Over the past fifty years, controlling the vast wealth created through taxation, they have built a huge federal, state and local bureaucracy which not only employs their own kind but implements a wealth of programs that reflects the wishes of their base, the unions, environmentalists, the gays, the feminists, abortionists, the anti war pacifists, etc. Through laws, they have dramatically increased their power and numbers and have done what socialist leader Norman Thomas predicted, many years ago, "The American people will never knowingly adopt socialism, but under the name of liberalism they will adopt every fragment of the socialist program until one day America will be a socialist nation without ever knowing how it happened."

Is all lost? Not by a long shot.

The leftists are increasingly having problems within their own Democrat ranks. The dissident splinter groups they've attracted and wooed began to make demands in the 1980's and 1990's. They had contributed to the Democrat victories, now they wanted their reward. They wanted more of their own kind openly elected to office and they wanted their issues enacted into law. Instead of being splinter groups kept in the closet, they demanded to be heard and their wishes subsequently, became part of our laws.

They got their wish and they, the dissonant, are now involved in helping run the Democrat Party. The tail is now wagging the old "Democratic" donkey. The anti-war, pro-abort, environmental extremists, anti-gun, anti-family, soft on crime, big spending liberals, feminists, and deviants of both sexes are calling the political tune and are marching hand in hand with the Democrat San Francisco leadership in gay and union parades. A large body of old rank and file democrats are finally scratching their heads and wondering, "What's going on?" Many of them hesitatively abandoned the jackass and climbed aboard the elephant when Reagan was in charge but would have nothing to do with the RINO's the Republican Party has offered them in recent elections.

Fortunately, a growing number of worried Americans are becoming aware of how it all happened. Trouble is, most know little about what to do about it outside of trying to inform their fellow Americans. There are many irritated and disturbed Americans anxious to do something—but what? Americans answered that problem by forming Tea Party groups in their local communities. Their success has been earth shaking, driving liberals to distraction by changing the political landscape in 2010 elections.

We must remember millions of Americans who are waking up still hold to the core traditional and religious values and are holding their noses to the political corruption that surrounds us. When properly informed and given good leadership, they will work diligently to see that the left in both parties are routed out and that we return to our traditional moral values and Constitutional government.

There is a truism in economic circles, "bad money drives out good." The same thing is true in politics. Bad people drive out good ones and that fact is really holding true. Bad Democrats are driving out good ones. In rural America, the trend is decidedly towards a return to basic American values. Who would have believed forty years ago, that below the Mason-Dixon Line, the South would turn Republican? Or that rock-ribbed Republican New Englander's would tolerate Barney Frank or Olympia Snow in office?

The left hasn't gained total control, for if they had, they'd have made it a "crime" for me to write what you have just read. There is little time and means to turn it all around and get the buggers out of government. They are still a minority but they hold some key reigns of governmental power. They're organized and in control and we are not—yet. I know it's possible to defeat the left, and so do they. The "progressives" are a small minority but tenacious, vicious, unprincipled and the most devious bunch of rascals who ever inculcated themselves into public office.

The difference is they are active in politics while Christians and most Americans are just waking up to their responsibilities. An awakened Christian citizenry terrifies the left. That is why, when recently challenged, and confronted, this thin veneer of gossamer wing civility rubs off for all to see. We are now starting to openly witness how uncivil and uncouth these pagans really are when threatened. It's a fight between the pagans and the patriots. It's a great complement they pay us when they lose their cool and vulgarly attack our character and beliefs. Let's happily look forward to more of it, bask in the criticism—it means we'll be winning.

Listen to the wisdom of Ben Franklin on the subject of personal attacks.

As to the abuses, I have met with, I number them among my honors. One cannot behave so as to obtain the esteem of the wise and good without drawing on one's self at the same time the envy and malice of the foolish and the wicked, and the latter is testimony of the former. The best men have always had their share of this treatment and the more of it in proportion to their different and greater degrees of merit. A man has therefore some reason to be ashamed of himself when he meets with none.

Epilogue

You can be a more effective spokesman for our Nation if you really wish to be. Anything that is worthwhile takes time and patience, and contrary to some doom peddlers, I believe we have the time to shape up this Nation—that is if we keep trying!

Totalitarianism is only inevitable when people accept the premise that defeat is inevitable.

You, the reader (yes, I mean you) have the responsibility to do something about it. If you don't like what's going on, stop griping and get active. There are hundreds of things that can be done. The first is to educate yourself properly, then develop the ability to communicate your knowledge, and work with others.

One rapid way to develop the ability to communicate your ideas is to secure a good friend, who believes as you do and then practice on each other. One of you should play the part of the "Liberal" and the other the "Conservative," then alternate. When you make a mistake, stop the discussion and analyze. You will be surprised how quickly you will develop good discussion habits. Also, you won't be alienating people while you learn.

One day you will find yourself in a conversation with a strong Liberal friend who formerly verbally boxed you around at will. This time, if you have developed good discussion techniques, you will find that he isn't as glib as you had thought.

He, for a change, is defending, and you are getting your points over, one after another. You will never forget this day, it will be a vintage day! You will find then that you will have more confidence in your ability to talk conservatism, and before long you will be confident enough to discuss your ideas with anyone.

"So you're a Liberal, ADA, ACLU, NAACP, CORE member, well, well, well. There's a question that I would like to ask you, and if you can keep to the subject we can, etc., etc., etc."

References

1. Hunter, Edward, "Communist Psychological Warfare [brain-washing]; House Committee on Un-American Activities; U.S. Government printing Office" Washington, March 13, 1958, pg. 12.

2. Ibid. pg 12 & 13.

3. Whittaker Chambers, "Witness" pg. 475.

4. Ibid.

5. Leonard Read. "Awake For Freedom's Sake" The Foundation For Economic Education, Inc. Irvington - on- the Hudson, New York.

6. Possony, Dr. Stefan T. "Language As A Communist Weapon" House Committee on Un-American Activities; U.S. Government Printing Office, Washington, March 2, 1959. p.3

7. Ibid. p 1

8. Ibid. pp 8 & 9

9. Ibid. pp.8 & 9

10. "McCarthy and His Enemies" William Buckley

11. "One Nation Under God" Rus Walton

12. Harry Dexter White. James Burnham's. "The Web of Subversion"

13. Alger Hiss. "The Web of Subversion" "Witness"

14. All these books can be purchased on Amazon.com

15. Robt. Morris. "No Wonder That We Are Losing" Amazon

16. Bastiat, Fredric, "The Law & Clichés of Socialism" Amazon

17. Hoover, J. Edger. "Masters of Deceit." Skousen, Cleon, "The Naked Communist"

    "You Can Trust the Communists" [to be communists] by Dr. Fred Swartz.

18. Lenin, V. I., Religion; "Little Lenin Library".

19. "Moulding Minds for the New China" London Times, May 16, 1956.

20. Ibid.

21. Sargant, William "Battle for the Mind."

22. Ibid. pg.59.

23. Ibid.

Classics - Great Reading!

"The Law"
Fredrick Bastiat

"Road to Serfdom"
Friedrich Hayek

"The Mainspring of Human Progress"
Henry Grady Weaver

"Masters of Deceit"
J. Edgar Hoover

"You Can Trust the Communists"
Dr. Fred Swartz

"Economics In One Lesson"
Henry Hazlitt

New Books

"Great Quotations that Shaped the Western World"
Carl Middleton

"Bringing America Home"
Tom Paukin

"One Nation Under God"
Dee Wampler

"Crimes Against Liberty"
David Limbaugh

"Saving Freedom"
U.S. Senator Jim DeMint

CPSIA information can be obtained at www.ICGtesting.com
Printed in the USA
BVOW040841280612

293896BV00001B/7/P